Eggs on Cheese.—Take half... cheese to two eggs and thr... of milk. Cut the chees... and put into a tin or dish... milk and eggs (well beat... moderate oven for about five... minutes. When done, serve h...

FRANCES.—(1) The following is a very simple recipe for shortbread, but it is a good one: Warm and cream half a pound of butter; add it to one pound of flour, stirring all the time; then add a quarter of a pound of sugar. Work the paste very smooth, roll out on a pasteboard to about half an inch thick, place in a greased tin, and bake for half an hour in a quick oven. (2) I think you write an excellent hand.

...s, Ludgat...

Lemon Pudding.—Ingredients: Half a pint of new milk, two ounces of bread-crumbs, one lemon, the yolks of four eggs, three ounces of butter, and five ounces of white sugar. Set the milk on the fire, and when it begins to boil put in the bread-crumbs. After boiling gently for two or three minutes add the butter and sugar, the juice and grated rind of a lemon, and the eggs, well beaten. Line a dish with puff paste, put in a layer of preserve, pour the mixture over it, and bake half an hour in moderately hot oven.

Little Buns.—Rub three ounces of butter into six ounces of flour; add three ounces of castor sugar, and half a teaspoonful of ground ginger. Make into stiff dough with one well-beaten egg and a little milk if required. Take a small piece on a fork, and roll in desiccated cocoanut; bake for twenty-minutes on a greased baking-sheet in a moderate oven.

In addition to those
published, here are two which seem to be
good :—

L. A. C., writing from Walsall, gives this—
½lb. ground rice, 4oz. carbonate of soda,
2oz. tartaric acid. Thoroughly mix and keep
dry.

Mr. G. S. (Pokesdown) says—Mix 7lb. of
flour, 2oz. cream of tartar, 1oz. carbonate of
soda ; pass through a sieve. This will keep,
in a dry, cool place, for any length of time.

Bed Sores
Castor oil
Balsam Peru
Balsam Copav.
equal parts of
to be applied warm
to the back.

Cure for Rheumatism
1. Sweet Oil
1. Turpentine
3. apodelaloc
3. Hartehorn
2. Stronger Ammonia
10. Add ½ wine
glass of vinegar.
Adams Dentist Iron
13306

Orange Pie.

Grate the rind of one and use the juice
of two large oranges; beat the yolks of
four eggs very light into two tablespoon-
fuls of butter and one heaping cup of sugar,
and put to the juice; add a little nutmeg
Beat all well together. Cover the pie-dish
with a thick paste, and pour this mixture
into it, and bake in a quick oven; when
done so it is like a finely baked custard; add
to the whites of the four eggs two table-
spoonfuls of white sugar and one of orange
juice. Cover this over the pie, and set back
into the oven till a light brown.

FARMHOUSE COOKERY
Laura Mason

 THE NATIONAL TRUST

ACKNOWLEDGEMENTS
Many people helped with ideas for this book. First, thanks are due to all who sent recipes, in particular Hazel Relph and people from the Lake District, where local pride is still expressed in good food and firmly rooted in tradition. I apologise to those whose recipes didn't make it into the final book. A huge thank you to Sandy Boyd, who patiently drove me around narrow country roads and provided lots of information and contacts. Other National Trust tenants and personnel who provided information, ideas and sometimes ingredients were Julia Horner, Nikki Exton, Ian and Denise Bell, Mark Russell, Rod Brake, Juliet Rogers and the Well-Hung Meat Company. Fionnuala Jay-O'Boyle and Nora Brown at Taste of Ulster were tremendously helpful, and Ben Watson at Riverford Farm Shop also assisted. I'd also like to thank, Fiona Quarmby, Beverley Cole and Joe and Emma Roberts. Finally, thanks to family and friends who gave practical help and discussed ideas, especially Ruth Grant, Andy and Angela Davidson, Alison and Steve Mummery, Anne Horn and Stella Hobbs.

First published in Great Britain in 2005
by National Trust Enterprises Limited,
36 Queen Anne's Gate, London, SW1H 9AS

www.nationaltrust.org.uk
Text © Laura Mason 2005
Food photography by Imagen.
Food photography © The National Trust 2005

ISBN 0 7078 0386 1

Designed by SMITH

Editorial and picture research by Helen Purchas
Colour origination by Digital Imaging Ltd. Glasgow
Printed and bound in Hong Kong by Printing Express Ltd.
Jacket. 'Hen and Chickens', detail from a nursery frieze from Lanhydrock, Cornwall, circa 1905, published by Lawrence and Jellicoe.

INTRODUCTION

This book celebrates two things: the tradition of farmhouse cookery, and the link between landscape and food, especially as it is experienced through food produced by the tenants of National Trust properties. The Trust is more than aristocratic houses, it manages farmland scattered across England, Wales and Northern Ireland. The model farm at Wimpole in East Anglia, the little fields of the Cornish coast, the deer-parks of the Welsh Marches, the mountains of Snowdonia and the Lake District fells have one thing in common, which is that they have been shaped over the centuries by food production. Beautiful landscapes may appear to be obvious and eternal combinations of grass, rock and water, but with a few exceptions this is an illusion. Much of their charm comes from precise systems of land use, for instance the distinctive pattern of herb-rich meadows stitched together by grey stone walls which has evolved through sheep- and cattle-raising in Upper Wharfedale, Yorkshire. The seemingly perfect vernacular buildings characteristic of such landscapes – great barns, isolated farmsteads, pleasingly composed hamlets or villages – are products of working on a human scale within the constraints of local materials. Food, either as raw ingredients or in particular recipes, could equally be seen as an expression of locality, of local taste working with available materials.

The original idea behind the recipes given here was to raise awareness of the activities of the Trust's farming tenants in the aftermath of the 2001 foot and mouth epidemic. During the epidemic farmers were faced with bans on livestock movements, which cut a major source of income, whilst media coverage and closure of footpaths adversely affected tourism, removing another. Some farmers began to market their produce directly, offering personal assurances of welfare standards and traceability. For many farmers this was a direct response to the difficulties imposed by the epidemic and a realisation that they produced interesting foods of excellent quality which deserved better than the small sums offered by the government during the emergency. Livestock farmers also had to think creatively when their farms became overstocked due to restrictions on the movement of animals.

As far as farmhouse cookery is concerned, it could be argued that farmers, like other people, rely on supermarkets for food. In the twenty-first century, the idea embraces a series of vague notions involving Aga cookers and bunches of cut herbs, gathering dust. Farmer's wives, diminishing in numbers along with farmers themselves, are more likely to be working in towns several miles away than making cheese and butter, raising poultry or preserving fruit. The cookery traditions of the countryside were gradually eroded by urbanisation in the nineteenth century, and then bastardised by the expediencies of rationing during the Second World War. They have been further diluted by supermarkets and disowned by most cookery writers. Despite this, there are people keeping ideas about traditional cookery and baking alive, and developing new sources of income for fragile, dwindling communities in the face of globalisation. Some of these people regularly cook recipes

(top) The Longhorn cow was a hardy breed extensively used in the north of England.
(bottom) Gathering the harvest was often a whole family affair.

which have been used by their families or in their regions for generations; others develop new ideas within the constraints of what their land produces and their own feelings of what is appropriate. Some of their recipes and ideas appear in this book. In addition, I have drawn on my own background as the child of a farming family. For other ideas, I have consciously looked back to before the Second World War. At this time several people made an effort to record traditional cookery, and I owe a debt to the work of Florence White, particularly *Good Things in England* (1932), the Women's Institute (W.I.) and Mrs Arthur Webb (who doesn't record her own Christian name) who toured the country in her car in the 1930s, writing columns for *Farmer's Weekly*. The work of more recent writers such as Theodora Fitzgibbon, Jane Grigson and Bobby Freeman has also provided ideas. Much of what was recorded in the 1920s and 1930s was of the 'good plain cooking' school – fine in the hands of good plain cooks supported by knowledgeable gardeners and tradesmen, but risky when practised by plain bad cooks using poor ingredients. The plainness was partly a response to the poverty which much of the population, urban and rural, endured during the nineteenth century; there is much evidence that earlier English food was both rich and well seasoned. At its best, the effect is a rustic simplicity of the type much admired when encountered in France or Italy, but belittled at home. I aimed for a balance between recipes still meaningful because they are rooted in a particular region and others which focus on local products. Some recipes have been left strictly alone,

whilst for others I have given more elaborate seasonings or altered their presentation, though not too much, as this is not a book of restaurant cookery, but nor is it a recipe museum. Tradition is not tradition unless it changes subtly, and some much-loved and symbolic foods, such as fruit cakes, have little to do with our landscapes. Yet they preserve memories of distant fashions, novelties and rituals in an edible form which has altered gradually over time.

The meals and dishes eaten in farmhouses have their own internal logic. This is how it appeared to one who grew up on a dairy farm in the Yorkshire Dales. You arose between five and six and had a cup of tea and a small bite to eat before getting on with the first milking. After two or three hours, you adjourned for a more substantial breakfast of porridge or cereal, bacon, eggs and toast or teacakes. The day's agenda was set by the season, but always involved much routine work and was punctuated by dinner, the biggest meal. Everyday dinners required good-tempered dishes such as stews and hot-pots which looked after themselves in a low oven, a necessity in busy households where most people were outdoors. These were made in large quantities for several workers whose exact numbers were sometimes unknown until the table was being set. They are also filling, another necessity when the company has been working in the open air in all weathers. Work in the afternoon depended partly on the season, with a lighter workload during the worst of the winter weather. Tea, in the late afternoon or early evening, after the second milking, usually brought the day to a close. Teas were important,

(above) During World War II traditional farming methods were eroded by the demands of providing food for the population.

A Welsh Mountain sheep from the Hafod y Llan estate in Snowdonia.

as they came at a time of day when one could generally expect to relax. Everyday teas were a miscellany of soup or eggs or cold meat or pies or salads, bread and lots of cakes. Baking to fill the cake tins was a major activity in a farmhouse kitchen. Special teas, for birthdays and social occasions such as club meetings or cricket matches, included numerous different types of sandwiches and fancy cakes.

Naturally this schedule varied, according to the season, family custom and region. The routines of growing grain demand more sustained bursts of outdoor work over several days, but not – as tractors replaced horses – consistently early starts, except at crucial times such as harvest. Raising sheep calls for long hours at lambing time and shearing. What all types of farming still have in common is a reliance on the right weather at the right time, and, despite mechanisation, a degree of exposure to the elements. The emphasis on meat, cream, butter and animal fats in many recipes may seem unhealthy; but these were the basics to hand, and the calorie-dense dishes reflected the appetites of those spending the best part of the day outdoors. A mango smoothie and plate of salad will not sustain a worker through a chilly day spent sorting sheep on a Lake District fell or drilling seed on the East Anglian fens. The food was not always heavy however. There were lighter dishes for summer, for special occasions and simply for variety, and some of these are also included. Inevitably, as all cookery writers do, I have picked the best and most interesting recipes, and some of the time food would be

plainer. Something which is as true for, say, rural France as it is for the Yorkshire Dales, but which tends to be overlooked in our culture of easy abundance.

Basic food traditions are national, but have regional nuances. Farmhouse traditions contain numerous variations on the theme of meat and potatoes, on small bread rolls and scones, and cakes large and small. The South West of England has a tradition of using pastry and clotted cream; the South East of puddings in suet crusts, and Wales of soupy stews and baking on the *planc*, an iron plate suspended over the fire. Baking from the Scottish Borders also featured the iron hotplate, here known as a griddle. The Lake District has a tradition of using brown sugar and spices derived from the West India trade once important to local harbours, whilst Yorkshire food included oatcakes, oatmeal parkin and home-baked bread. Fruit and vegetables were particularly regional, with emphasis on apples and cider in the South West and East Anglia, orchard fruit generally in Kent, and apples, pears and plums in the West Midlands. The north relied more on gooseberries and rhubarb, with damsons in the Lake District. Most kitchen gardens included potherbs such as leeks, cabbage and onions, but special items such as asparagus and watercress were grown as crops in limited areas. Differences between regions come from cooking methods, availability of ingredients, local tastes and survivals of items which were once the height of fashion but which have been forgotten everywhere except in one small corner of the country. Most of the recipes require little in the way of special equipment

(above) A cartoon of Joseph Arch from *Vanity Fair* 1886. A former agricultural labourer, Arch founded the National Union of Farm Labourers in 1872.

'Knights Earl' black cherries from *Lindley's British Fruit 1846*.

A DARWINIAN IDEA.
SUGGESTED BY THE CATTLE SHOW.

THE OLD SORT.

THE MODERN IMPROVEMENT.

WHAT IT MUST COME TO.

or ingredients; where this is needed it is specified. Here are a few pointers which will help with some of the recipes.

Yeast: this is easily available in dried form. All yeasted recipes in this book have been tested with dried active yeast which is 'started' by adding the required amount to warm, sweetened liquid and leaving it to stand for 10 minutes or so until frothy. The easy blend type, which is mixed with the dry ingredients, works for plain doughs, but I have not found it successful for rich mixtures containing cream, butter or eggs.

Rennet: rennet is an enzyme that curdles milk. Originally derived from calves' stomachs; the rennet commonly sold now is cultured using microbes and is a vegetarian product. Once opened, store in the fridge. It will lose its strength gradually, taking longer to set milk, so try to use it fairly quickly. Milk for rennetting should be at blood heat, and once the rennet is added do not disturb until set.

Lining a pudding basin with suet crust: form the pastry into a ball and roll out to a thickness of almost 1cm ($^1/_2$ in). Cut out a quarter circle and set aside. Paint the edges of the pastry with cold water, then ease into the basin making a neat seam up the edge where the section was removed. Take the reserved piece of pastry and re-roll it into a small circle. Add the filling to the basin, paint the edge of the smaller circle with water, and use it as a lid,

sealing round the edges as before. Trim the pastry and cover with a double layer of foil or greaseproof paper, with a pleat to allow for the pudding to expand during cooking. Tie securely round the brim of the basin with string and make a loop over the top to form a handle.

For vegetarians: many recipes, call for butter, lard or suet. Margarine, block vegetable fat designed for baking and vegetarian suet can be used instead.

Basic shortcrust pastry: the basic rule for shortcrust pastry is to use half the weight of fat to flour. The type of fat used affects the flavour and texture. Lard produces a very short pastry, butter gives a pastry which is less short but has a good flavour. Many cooks favour a mixture of the two. Solid vegetable fat and margarine can both be used for pastry making, but reduced fat and low fat spreads are unsuitable.

300g/10$^1/_2$ oz flour mixed with a generous pinch of salt
150g/5$^1/_2$ oz butter, lard or butter and lard mixed
6–8 tablespoons of cold water

Put the flour and salt in a bowl. Cut the fat into 1cm/$^1/_2$ in cubes and add to the flour. Rub the fat into the flour until the mixture resembles fine breadcrumbs. Add sufficient water to make a coherent dough, a little more or less may be needed. Shape into a ball, wrap in cling film and put in a cool place for at least 30 minutes to rest before using.

(top) This cartoon from *Punch* in 1865 highlights concerns with contemporary farming 'improvements'.

CORNWALL

Cornwall may be Britain's southernmost county, but that doesn't mean the climate is easy. 'We get salt gales here which kill the nettles', says Rod Brake, a tenant on National Trust land near Porth Mawgan. Mr Brake's farm is on a cliff-top and in January that means horizontal rain mixed with salt spray from the sea pounding the rocks below. It's not especially cold, but it's tough. The wind and the rain it sweeps in off hundreds of miles of uninterrupted ocean is a force to be reckoned with for much of the year.

By the time most visitors get there, in summer, the fields have become soft and green, the sea has calmed down, and they wonder why hedges are planted on top of granite walls which obscure the view and are unforgiving for the careless or inattentive driver. They are windbreaks, offering a little protection to both man and beast. There aren't many trees, and the ones that are there lean away from the west at forty-five degree angles, even on the south coast.

On three sides Cornwall rises out of the sea, mostly as steep cliffs. On top the land is surprisingly level. In the south-western part of the county the cliffs are softened in places by the Fowey and Carrick Roads, hung with trees and many-coloured little towns like a child's paintbox. Otherwise, the traditional architecture has a stern, small-windowed simplicity which reflects the hard building stone and the need to exclude wind and rain. Roofs are slate, not thatch. On the fourth side the county shares a boundary

(previous page) Kynance Cove, Cornwall
(above) A panoramic view of Godolphin Hill, Cornwall.

with Devon, marked for much of its length by the River Tamar. It is a mistake to think of Cornwall as a purely agricultural landscape; it has been mined for tin in the south-west, for china clay in the St Austell area and for smooth charcoal-grey slate at Delabole.

How does this particular combination of rain and wind, soil and grass, of scattered farms and little semi-industrial mining communities and fishing towns express itself in food? To the summer tourist, the most obvious items are pasties, clotted cream and fish. The climate is not especially conducive to growing corn, and historically barley bread was more important than wheat. Possibly locally grown wheat flour was more suitable for pastry; there are certainly numerous traditional pastry dishes in Cornish cookery books, although Cornish saffron cake, really a type of fruit bread, has a long history. A vegetable and herb tradition is apparent in some of the fillings cited for pasties and pies: leeks, parsley and the more general catch-all of 'herbs'. The relatively mild temperatures and good soils of the south-westernmost part of the county produce excellent early potatoes and other vegetables. Whilst most fields are pretty much square, on the north coast traces of medieval strip systems have been fossilised in patterns of grass and hedgerow – these are known as 'stitchfields' and are particularly apparent at Forrabury Stitches above Boscastle, but can also be glimpsed elsewhere.

Grazing sheep and cattle for meat production is also very important. Several National Trust tenants use traditional animal breeds in land management schemes, such as Manx

Loaghtan sheep or Devon cattle grazed on the cliffs east of the Fowey estuary, in an attempt to encourage bio-diversity. Somehow, magically, this slightly unpromising landscape also produces clotted cream, one of the richest and most unctuous of British dairy produce, for which Cornwall is justly famous. Cheesemaking, whilst never as strong a tradition as in Somerset, has benefited from the creativity of the past few decades and Cornish Yarg has become respected as a new cheese and a local speciality. Finally, the sea itself provided employment for sailors and fishermen and brought sources of food beyond those of just the land. Fish is often combined in the cream and pastry tradition, and although it is not produce of the land as such, a recipe has been included here because fishermen and farmers live side by side in this area.

(top) Traditional stone wall, near Newquay, Cornwall.
(bottom) A tin mine chimney stack atop Cape Cornwall.

LAMB STEAKS WITH QUINCE

Mark and Charlotte Russell raise delicious lamb at Lanteglos, near Fowey. They sell some at their farm but to buy steaks you'll have to go to Devon, to Riverford Farm Shop, Staverton near Totnes where Ben Watson seams the leg meat into individual muscles. He suggested this way of cooking them.

Serves 4

- a little olive oil
- 8 shallots, peeled and sliced
- 4 garlic cloves, peeled and sliced
- a sprig of rosemary
- 25g/1oz butter
- 4 leg steaks, each weighing about 150–200g/5½–7oz If you can't buy neat, lean steaks use neck fillet, cut in slices.
- 200ml/7fl oz light stock, chicken or beef
- 60ml/2½ fl oz double cream
- 40g/1½ oz quince jelly or paste – if very stiff, soften in a little warm water
- salt, pepper and a little lemon juice

Put a little olive oil in a small saucepan. Add the shallots, garlic and rosemary and cook slowly until soft. Drain off any excess oil and discard the rosemary.

Melt half the butter in a large frying pan. When hot, add the lamb steaks and fry rapidly on both sides until done to your taste. Remove to a heated plate and keep warm whilst you make the sauce. Add the remaining butter and the cooked shallots. Fry quickly, then add the garlic and cook a little longer, but don't let it brown. Add the stock, turn up the heat and cook rapidly until syrupy. Stir in the cream and let it amalgamate. Then add the quince jelly and cook, stirring for a few moments to mix thoroughly. Taste, correct the seasoning and add a squeeze of lemon juice if the quince jelly is on the bland side. Serve with the steaks.

CHICKEN AND PARSLEY PIE

A dish which is recorded in both Devon and Cornwall, always, it seems, as a very large pie made from two chickens. Delicious both hot and cold. You can ask your butcher to joint and skin the chicken for you.

Serves 8

- 2 chickens, the meat cut off and divided into neat joints and skinned. Use the bones and skin to make stock, a little of which is needed for the pie.
- salt, pepper and nutmeg
- flour for dusting
- 1 large bunch of parsley picked off the stems, chopped
- 4 shallots, finely chopped
- 100g/3½ oz cooked ham or bacon, cut in dice
- 250ml/8½ fl oz chicken stock
- 2 quantities of shortcrust pastry (see page 13)
- 250ml/8½ fl oz double cream

A deep pie dish of a suitable size and a pie funnel

Season the chicken joints with pepper, salt and a scrape of nutmeg. Dust with flour. Put a layer of parsley and some shallot in the bottom of the pie dish, and cover with chicken pieces. Scatter the ham or bacon and the remaining parsley and shallot over then fill up the dish with chicken. Insert the pie funnel in the middle. Add the stock to fill up the dish to about the halfway mark. Roll out the pastry and cover the pie. Make a hole in the centre to accommodate the pie funnel, and a pastry rose to cover it.

Bake at 220°C/425°F/gas mark 7 for 20 minutes, then lower the heat to 170–180°C/325–350°F/gas mark 3–4 and cook for another 60–75 minutes. At the end of the cooking time, heat the cream to boiling. Ease off the rose and pour into the pie. Serve very hot, or allow to go completely cold and chill.

A familiar ingredient throughout the medieval period, quinces are increasingly popular today.

CORNWALL

PASTIES

Pasties - or oggies - are made all over Cornwall but the quality varies, to put it politely. Made with fresh ingredients and good meat, they are a fine thing.

Makes 2 large pasties

- 1 quantity shortcrust pastry (see page 13)
- 200g/7oz potato, peeled and chopped
- 100g/3¹/₂oz raw turnip, chopped
- 60g/2oz onion, chopped
- 250–300g/9–10¹/₂oz steak chuck or skirt, finely chopped (don't use minced beef)
- milk or egg to glaze

Make the pastry using the recipe on page 13.Let it rest for about 30 minutes, then roll out to 5mm/¹/₂in thick and cut two dinner plate-sized rounds. Mix the vegetables and use to cover half of each piece of pastry. Season the meat well and cover the vegetables. Wet the edges of the pastry, fold each piece in half and crimp the edges; brush with milk or beaten egg to glaze. Bake on a lightly greased tray, starting in a hot oven 200°C/400°F/gas mark 6. After 15 minutes, lower the heat to 180°C/350°F/gas mark 4 and cook for another 45 minutes.

CORNISH FISH PIE

Cornish farmhouse traditions mix fish and dairy produce. Fresh sea bass is in season between August and March, however smaller farmed fish are available all year round. Ask your fishmonger for some bones and trimmings for stock.

Serves 4

- 450g/1lb sea bass fillets, skinned
- a little butter for greasing
- salt, pepper
- 1 tablespoon of parsley, chopped
- 60ml/2¹/₂fl oz fish stock
- 1 quantity shortcrust pastry made with butter and lard mixed (see page 13)
- 100ml/3¹/₂fl oz single cream
- 2 tablespoons clotted cream

A pie dish which will hold the fish neatly

Cover the fish bones and trimmings with water and simmer gently for 20 minutes to produce a little fish stock. Cut the fish fillets into slices about 3cm/1¹/₂in wide. Grease the pie dish and lay the fish in it. Scatter salt, pepper and chopped parsley over. Add the fish stock.

Roll out the pastry and top the pie with it, trimming neatly. Cut a hole in the centre and make a pastry rose to cover it. Bake the pie for about 15 minutes at 220°C/425°F/gas mark 7. Warm the single cream gently until almost boiling. Lift the pastry rose and pour the warmed cream into the pie. Return to the oven for another five minutes. Just before serving, lift the crust at the edge and place the clotted cream over the fish.

BACON AND SPINACH PIE

This is another example of the Cornish habit of enclosing everything in pastry.

Serves 4

- 250g/9oz bacon rashers
- 3–4 shallots, finely chopped
- 250g/9oz spinach
- 1 bunch of watercress, chopped
- 1 handful of parsley, chopped
- 2 eggs, beaten
- 30–50ml/1–2fl oz single cream pepper
- 1 quantity shortcrust pastry made with butter and lard mixed (see page 13)

Trim the bacon rashers of any excess fat and use a little of this to soften the chopped shallot in a frying pan. Blanch the spinach by plunging it into boiling water and draining well, put it in a sieve and press to remove excess water.

Use a third of the bacon to line the base of a pie dish. Cover with half the chopped spinach, scatter half the watercress and parsley over, then add the softened shallots. Cover with another third of the bacon, then add the rest of the greenery. Beat the eggs with the cream and a little pepper but no salt – the bacon will probably provide enough, and pour over. Top with the rest of the bacon. Roll out the pastry, cover the dish and crimp the edges. Bake at 170°C/325°F/gas mark 3 for 1 hour. Serve hot.

Salvia Officinalis, or sage, has been revered as a healing plant for centuries.

ROAST GOOSE WITH SAGE AND ONION STUFFING

Mr and Mrs Hunn rear geese and turkeys for Christmas at Saltash. This is the classic English way with geese. Ask your butcher to retain the giblets, but exclude the liver.

Serves 6

- 1 goose with giblets, weighing about 4½ kg/10lb

For the stuffing
- 1 large onion, finely chopped
- 80g/3oz fresh sage leaves, finely chopped
- 300g/10½oz fresh white breadcrumbs
- 1 teaspoon salt
- zest of ½ lemon
- generous amount of freshly ground black pepper
- 1 egg

For the gravy
- 2 rashers bacon, cut in strips
- ½ an onion, chopped
- 1 carrot, chopped
- 2 sticks of celery, chopped
- goose giblets
- 1 bay leaf
- 75ml/2½fl oz brandy
- 1 heaped teaspoon cornflour

To make the stuffing, mix the onion and the sage leaves with the breadcrumbs. Add the salt and lemon zest and grind in plenty of pepper. Use the egg to bind the mixture. Remove any visible lumps of fat from inside the goose (render them down for roasting potatoes) and spoon in the stuffing.

Put the goose on a wire rack in a large baking tin and rub the skin with salt. Roast at 200°C/400°F/gas mark 6 for 2½ –3 hours, occasionally pouring off the fat which accumulates in the roasting tin.

To make the gravy, cook the bacon gently until the fat runs. Chop the vegetables and add to the bacon along with the giblets. Brown these, then add the bay leaf, cover with water and leave to simmer gently, allowing the liquid to reduce by about a third.

When the goose is cooked, remove it to a warm plate and leave to rest. Pour off the fat in the roasting tin. Add the brandy and let it bubble, scraping to take up any sediment. Strain in the stock from the giblets and bring to the boil. Taste and adjust the seasoning. Mix a generous teaspoon of cornflour with a little water and stir into the gravy, heating again until the mixture has thickened.

'Buy my goose, my fat goose!' from *Cries of London*, Thomas Rowlandson, 1799.

CELERY SAUCE FOR TURKEY

Most people think of roast when they think of turkey, and celery sauce would be good with this, but it is really intended to go with boiled turkey - if you want to try the combination, simmer a small turkey (about 5kg/11lb) in water with the usual potherbs (leeks, carrots and onions), for about 1½ hours. When it's done, the leg will start to part easily from the body.

- 1 head of celery, trimmed, leaves removed, thinly sliced
- 850ml/1½ pints of light stock (made from veal, chicken or the turkey giblets)
- 60g/2½ oz butter, softened
- 40g/1½ oz plain flour
- 100ml/3½ fl oz single cream
- salt and pepper
- fresh tarragon, chopped (optional)

Simmer the celery in the stock for about 20 minutes. Mix the butter and flour together and add to the stock and celery in small bits. Stir well, keeping the temperature just below boiling, until the mixture thickens. Add the cream and season with salt and pepper, and a little chopped tarragon if you like.

CORNISH POTATO CAKES

Floury maincrop potatoes are necessary for these tasty cakes.

Makes approx.18

- 2–3 floury potatoes, total weight 500g/1lb 2oz, boiled in the skins and allowed to cool (but they must not be chilled)
- 60g/2½ oz beef suet
- 60g/2½ oz plain flour
- 1 teaspoon baking powder
- a generous pinch of salt

Peel the potatoes and crumble them into small pieces. Mix with the other ingredients to make a smooth, slightly sticky paste. Don't overwork it. Roll the paste out on a well-floured work surface to a thickness of 1cm/½ in. Cut into squares. Bake at 200°C/400°F/gas mark 6 for 10–15 minutes until browned and crisp. Eat immediately.

CORNISH SPLITS
Small bread rolls are made all over Britain. This is a Cornish version as recorded by Florence White in the 1930s. These little rolls are delicious with clotted cream and jam.

- 1 tablespoon dried yeast
- 1 teaspoon granulated sugar
- 60ml/2½ fl oz hand-hot milk
- 120g/4oz butter, plus a little extra for greasing
- 25g/1oz lard
- 750g/1lb 10oz strong plain flour
- 1 teaspoon salt
- 400ml/14fl oz tepid water

Cream the yeast with the sugar in the warm milk. Gently melt the butter and lard and add to the flour, together with the yeast mixture. Sprinkle in the salt. Add enough of the tepid water to make a dough. Knead for about 10 minutes, cover and put in a warm place to rise. When doubled in size, knock back and knead again. Divide into 50g/1½ oz pieces and make into rolls. Place on a greased baking tray and allow to prove. Bake at 220°C/425°F/gas mark 7 for 20 minutes. On removing the rolls from the oven, rub over with a butter paper and then wrap in a cloth to cool.

A view of the ancient radial field patterns at Rosemergy Farm, Cornwall.

BUBBLE AND SQUEAK SOUP

This is good for showing off the potatoes and cabbage which southern Cornwall grows in vast amounts. The basic recipe closely follows Portuguese _caldo verde_. For a vegetarian version, omit the bacon and use a little extra butter.

Serves 6

- 25g/1oz butter
- 120g/4oz bacon, cut in matchsticks
- 1/2 a medium onion, finely chopped
- 900g/2lb maincrop potatoes, peeled and cut in chunks
- 200g/7oz spring cabbage, finely sliced
- salt and pepper
- 100ml/3 1/2 fl oz single cream

Melt the butter in a large pan and add the bacon. Cook gently until crisp, then remove and set aside. Add the onion to the fat and cook gently until soft but not brown. Add the potatoes and 1 litre/1 3/4 pints water. Simmer until the potatoes are soft, then use a potato masher to break them down.

Discard the biggest outside leaves of the cabbage, plus any torn or discoloured bits and the chunkiest parts of the stems. Wash thoroughly and cut the largest leaves in half lengthways. Roll several leaves together in a tight roll and slice finely. Add it to the basic soup. Season well. Cook gently for another 7–10 minutes until the cabbage is tender. Add the cream and serve with a scattering of the bacon pieces in each bowl.

FRANKLIN'S POTATOES

Based on a dish from the 1920s, this is an English take on the _gratin_. It needs waxy potatoes – the new potatoes grown in south Cornwall are perfect. Serve with roast chicken or game as a change from roast potatoes.

Serves 6–8

- 500ml/18fl oz milk
- 2 shallots, peeled and cut in quarters
- 8 whole cloves
- 50g/2oz fine white breadcrumbs, plus 25g/1oz or so for finishing the dish
- salt, pepper
- a little mace and a pinch of chilli
- 1–2 tablespoons single cream (optional)
- 900g/2lb medium new potatoes
- butter for greasing

A 1.7-litre/3-pint soufflé dish or similar

Heat the milk, the shallots and the cloves to boiling point. Turn off the heat and leave to infuse for at least 30 minutes. Then strain the milk into a clean pan and add the breadcrumbs. Heat gently for few minutes, stirring, until you have a smooth bread sauce. Season rather highly with salt, pepper and spices and add the cream if desired.

Scrub and scrape the potatoes if the skins are easy to remove – otherwise leave them and peel after boiling. Leave the potatoes whole. Cover with cold water, bring to the boil and cook for 10–15 minutes: they should be half-cooked. Drain and leave until cool enough to handle. Remove any patches of skin and slice into rounds about as thick as a pound coin.

Thin the bread sauce, which will have thickened up, with a little extra milk and use a couple of ladlefuls to cover the base of the buttered dish. Add a layer of potato slices and continue layering sauce and potatoes until used up, finishing with potatoes. Sprinkle the extra breadcrumbs over the top. Bake at 190°C/375°F/gas mark 5 for about an hour.

SAFFRON CAKE

Not a cake in the modern sense, but a fruit bread lightly spiced with saffron, and traditionally Cornish.

- a generous pinch of saffron threads
- 3 tablespoons boiling water
- 500g/1lb 2oz strong plain white flour
- 1 tablespoon dried yeast
- 100ml/3 1/2 fl oz tepid water
- 100g/3 1/2 oz lard or butter
- 1 teaspoon salt
- 100g/3 1/2 oz sugar
- 1 egg, beaten
- 250g/9oz currants
- 30g/1 1/4 oz chopped candied peel

A 1.2litre/2-pint loaf tin, greased

Put the saffron in the boiling water and leave to infuse overnight. Mix 100g/3 1/2 oz flour, a pinch of sugar, the yeast and the tepid water, and leave it for about 30 minutes until frothy.

Rub the fat into the remaining flour. Add the salt, sugar and egg, the yeast mixture and the saffron water. Mix to a coherent dough, adding a little more tepid water as necessary. Knead well, cover the bowl with cling film and leave to rise in a warm place for about an hour.

Knock back and knead in the fruit and peel. Place in the greased loaf tin and prove for about an hour.

Bake at 220°C/425°F/gas mark 7 for 40 minutes, or until the loaf sounds hollow when tapped on the base. Cool on a wire rack. Eat thinly sliced, spread with butter.

MY LADY'S SHORTCAKE

Under this name, Mrs Arthur Webb gave instructions for one of our numerous variations on the theme of currants and pastry. It seems to be a relative of a Cornish cake known as 'heavy cake' or 'hevvas' – a concoction of butter or cream, flour and currants, but is lighter and more delicate.

- 200g/7oz plain flour
- 100g/3 1/2 oz butter
- 60g/2oz mixed peel
- 60g/2oz currants
- 60g/2oz sultanas
- 2 tablespoons caster sugar
- egg to glaze

Use the flour, butter and a little cold water to make up some shortcrust pastry (see page 13). Allow it to rest for 30 minutes in the fridge, then roll it into a neat square about 30 x 30cm (12 x 12in). It should be quite thin. Scatter the peel, currants and sultanas over the top, then sprinkle the sugar over. Turn in 1cm/1/4in of pastry along each edge to contain the filling, then roll the pastry up like a swiss roll. Roll out again, gently so that the fruit doesn't break the surface too much, to give an oblong of roughly the same dimensions as the original. Score the surface to give a diamond pattern.

Bake at 220°C/425°F/gas mark 7 for 10 minutes, then turn the oven down to 180°C/350°F/gas mark 4 and bake for another 15 minutes. Around 5 minutes before the end of cooking, brush the top with beaten egg so that it has a nice glaze.

The ruins of Trewethet Mill, Tintagel, Cornwall.

KATHLEEN'S CORNISH FAIRINGS

Sara Paston-Williams quoted this recipe from Kathleen Stevens, who worked as a maid at Lanhydrock House, in *Jams, Preserves and Edible Gifts*.

- 2 level tablespoons golden syrup
- 225g/8oz butter
- 175g/6oz caster sugar
- 350g/12oz self-raising flour
- 1 teaspoon bicarbonate of soda
- 2 teaspoons ground ginger

In a large pan, melt the syrup and butter together over a low heat. Remove from the heat and stir in the sugar. Sieve the flour, bicarbonate of soda and ginger together into the pan, then stir together to form a dough. Roll into small balls, each the size of a walnut, and place on greased baking trays, leaving plenty of room between each one, as they spread during cooking. Bake at 180°C/350°F/gas mark 4 for 10 minutes or until golden brown and well spread. Leave to cool on the trays for a few minutes, then transfer to a wire rack to cool completely. Store in an airtight container.

CLOTTED CREAM AND BLACKBERRY RIPPLE ICE

The basic clotted cream ice is from Caroline Liddel and Robin Weir's *Ices: the definitive guide*.

For the blackberry ripple
- 500g/1lb 2oz blackberries
- 150g/5 $^1/_2$ oz sugar

For the custard
- 375ml/13fl oz milk
- 120g/4oz granulated sugar
- 5 egg yolks
- 125ml/4fl oz clotted cream

Put the blackberries in a saucepan with enough water to cover the base. Cook gently until they have yielded all their juice. Run through a sieve, discarding the berries. Measure 150ml/5fl oz of juice, combine with the sugar and bring to the boil. Set aside to cool.

Combine the milk and half the sugar in a medium-sized saucepan and bring to just below boiling point. Combine the egg yolks with the remaining sugar and beat until the mixture is pale and thick enough to hold the shape when a ribbon of mix is trailed across the surface. Pour the hot milk in a steady stream onto the egg and sugar mixture, beating steadily. Place the bowl over a pan of simmering water and allow to thicken (this may take up to 30 minutes, depending on the thickness of the bowl). Stir frequently. When the mixture coats the back of a wooden spoon and holds a clear shape when a horizontal line is drawn across the back of the spoon, it is thick enough. Remove the bowl and plunge the base into cold water to stop it cooking further. Then stir in the clotted cream. Allow to cool, stirring occasionally, then chill.

To freeze: if using an electric ice cream machine, churn the cream mix for a maximum of 10 minutes (no longer, or it will become buttery), then scrape the mixture quickly into a plastic freezer box. Add some of the blackberry/sugar mixture, which will probably have gelled but it doesn't matter, and marble it through the semi-frozen ice cream. Transfer to the freezer for an hour to harden up. Without a machine, turn out the cream mix in a freezer box, cover and put in the coldest part of the freezer. After an hour, scrape the ice that has formed round the edge to the centre of the mixture and beat for a few seconds with an electric hand beater to form a uniform slush. Return to the freezer.

Repeat the process after another hour. If the mixture seems reasonably well set at this point, marble the blackberry mixture through; if not, repeat the stirring process once more and then add the fruit. Allow to freeze until set.

Give the ice about 15 minutes to soften before serving if it has been frozen solid.

MRS PALMER'S RUSSIAN CREAM

Gillian Palmer, from Lanteglos near Fowey, remarks that this recipe was 'a great favourite with the teams of men who followed the threshing machines around the farms' in the early twentieth century. Similar dishes have been made in Britain since at least the eighteenth century, and don't seem to have much to do with Russia. It's well worth experimenting with different flavourings. Try a little lemon zest or a few drops of vanilla essence.

Serves 6

- 500ml/18fl oz full-fat milk
- 2 eggs, separated
- 100g/3 ½ oz caster sugar
- drops of vanilla essence or a little lemon zest
- 1 packet of powdered gelatine

Put the milk into a saucepan. Add the egg yolks, sugar, flavouring if used, and sprinkle the gelatine over. Stir well to break up the egg yolks, distribute the gelatine well, and put over a low heat. Meanwhile, whisk the egg whites to a stiff foam.

Increase the heat and bring just to the boil, stirring all the time (don't worry if it shows signs of curdling). Remove from the heat and stir the beaten egg whites through the mixture. Turn into a heatproof bowl and leave overnight in a cool place.

To serve, put a plate over the bowl, invert and shake gently. The pudding should slide out, and will have a clear jelly layer and a foamy layer. Serve with clotted cream.

RASPBERRY CREAM

A recipe based on one from a cookery manuscript dated 1847, belonging to the National Trust.

Serves 4–6

- 350g/12oz raspberries
- 70g/2 ½ oz caster sugar
- 2 tablespoons brandy
- 250ml/8 ½ fl oz double cream
- mint sprigs

Set aside a few of the nicest raspberries for a garnish. Rub the rest of the berries through a sieve, discarding the pips. Mix the raspberry purée with the sugar and brandy; put about a tablespoon of this into the bottom of each glass. Add the cream to the remainder and beat until stiff. Spoon into the glasses on top of the purée. Decorate with mint sprigs and the whole raspberries. Chill.

Cows grazing at Nanjulian Farm, Cornwall. The farm and its produce are entirely organic.

DEVON

After the tough, windswept plateau of Cornwall, south Devon feels like a duvet. Past the Tamar Valley, green with moss and ivy hung trees, the countryside is rounded and softer. The wind is less fierce than in Cornwall. The buildings follow the soft shapes of the cob and thatch tradition, and are tucked away in the folds of deep valleys, known as combes. Access to the coombes is down steep narrow lanes outlined by high, parallel banks, hung with hartshorn ferns. Sometimes the walls that wind along the village lanes are capped with thatch as well.

Not all of Devon is so gentle. The hills rise in ridges, gradually losing their enclosed feeling until they meet Dartmoor, a horizon of pointed granite tors which reach heights of over 400m (1,300ft) and catch the snow in winter. Dartmoor must always have been difficult to farm and is now marginal to agriculture, although prehistoric field systems hidden beneath the bracken, heather and scrub show that people have tried to farm it. From here the land is sparsely populated, rising north to Exmoor, a slab of peat-capped red sandstone emerging steeply out of the sea. Both environments are only suitable for rough grazing and game such as red deer. North Devon feels somewhat like a

(previous page) View of Woody Bay, Devon.
(above) The vivid colours of Countisbury Hill and Lynmouth, Devon.

continuation of Cornwall. The vegetation may be softer, a little less harassed by the wind and salt, but rain, in huge quantities, influences this landscape, as the deep gorges, and occasional dramatic floods, such as that at Lynmouth in the 1950s, demonstrate.

The varied landscape, from the soft climate of the sheltered south coast to the grass and heather tops of Exmoor, has given rise to two breeds of cattle, both a deep rich red. North Devons are hairy and tough beef cattle originally developed for the rough grazing of Exmoor. The Channel-Island influenced South Devons are dairy cattle, which contribute to the clotted cream and butter tradition so essential to perceptions of the county. Cheese, historically, was of less importance, although both Cheddar-style cheese and some continental-influenced cheeses are made.

The native sheep breed is the hardy Dartmoor. Both sheep and cattle produce good meat; some of it grazed on Trust land adjacent to the Salcombe estuary. Pigs also become more important. Devon cures for ham are usually brine based rather than dry salt. '*You* try and stop it turning into brine', a Devon farmer's wife once said to me, in acknowledgement of the humid climate.

The soft climate is good for potatoes and other vegetables, although few distinctive recipes appear to exist for them. Soft fruit such as strawberries also do well, after all, one has to have something to eat with the clotted cream. The south-western apple and cider tradition is very strong. Apples were used in some meat dishes recorded in the first half of the twentieth century, such as pies of

mutton and onions. These seem to have vanished, and possibly needed the slow heat of a brick bread oven to make them really well. The little bread rolls made in Cornwall under the name of splits were recorded in Devon as chudleighs, but seem to have been overtaken by scones as a basis for strawberry jam and clotted cream. The latter are also eaten with good Dartmoor heather honey or with golden syrup, a combination known as 'thunder and lightning'. As in Cornwall, cream and butter are also used as an enriching ingredient for pies, although the habit of putting everything in pastry becomes less pronounced.

(top) Close-up detail of a stone wall on Dartmoor, Devon.
(bottom) Wild grasses and flowers in a field of barley in Lydford Gorge, Devon.

POT ROAST BRISKET WITH SUMMER VEGETABLES

All those involved with marketing their own farm's meat remark that no one seems to want brisket. Strange, because it has a lovely flavour and makes wonderful gravy.

Serves 4–6

- dripping, oil or bacon fat
- 1kg /2 $\frac{1}{4}$ lb boned and rolled brisket
- 1 bunch spring onions, chopped
- 1 clove garlic, crushed
- 150ml/5fl oz red wine
- 200g/7oz young carrots, topped and tailed (if they are really young, they won't need peeling)
- 1 sprig of thyme
- 1 teaspoon of salt and some pepper
- 100g/3 $\frac{1}{2}$ oz peas (after podding)
- 150–200g/5 $\frac{1}{2}$ –7oz green beans, cut in short lengths
- 2 teaspoons cornflour or arrowroot

Use a pot that will hold the meat neatly. Melt a little fat and brown the meat all over. Remove to one side, add the spring onions and garlic to the fat and cook gently. When they have softened a bit, pour in the red wine and let it boil for a minute or two. Add the carrots and thyme and sit the meat on top. Sprinkle the salt and pepper. Cover the pot with foil and a lid and cook on a very low heat, or in a low oven at 170°C/325°F/gas mark 3 for about 2 $\frac{1}{2}$ hours.

At this point, uncover the pot. The meat will have produced lots of gravy. Add the peas and beans. Seal up again and continue to cook for another 30–40 minutes. Remove the meat to a warm dish. Skim the gravy if it seems to have a lot of fat on top. Slake the cornflour or arrowroot with a little cold water and add to the gravy, bring to the boil and stir whilst it thickens. Taste and correct the seasoning.

BILL'S BURGERS

There's a lot of very good lamb and beef production on Trust land in the Salcombe area. Photographer Bill Butt put his burger recipe on the Well-Hung Meat Company website (www.wellhungmeat.com), and all parties have kindly allowed me to quote it.

Makes approx. 5 burgers

- 100g/3 oz shallots
- 2 or 3 garlic cloves
- 1 handful fresh coriander
- 1 handful fresh thyme (strip the woodiest stalks out)
- 1kg/2 $\frac{1}{4}$ lb lean minced beef
- 1 egg beaten, and breadcrumbs for binding (optional)
- 1 teaspoon salt

Finely chop the shallots, garlic, coriander and thyme. Mix them in with the mince then scrunch together in balls of around 200g/7oz before flattening them into burgers. A little egg and breadcrumbs can help bind the burgers but this is not necessary. Stir in the salt then place the burgers under a hot grill or on a griddle and cook to your preference. I'd also add a good teaspoon of salt to the mixture.

A sculpture celebrating the Red Devon Ox at Buckland Abbey. The sculpture is made of steel and was designed by Jonathan Rodney-Jones in 2000.

BEEF IN BRANSCOMBE BITTER

The National Trust owns a brewery at Branscombe in Devon. I used their Drayman's Best bitter, a smooth, hoppy beer, for this casserole.

Serves 4

- 3 tablespoons plain flour
- salt and pepper
- 600g/1lb 5oz shin of beef, thickly sliced
- 30g/1 1/4 oz butter or 2 tablespoons oil
- 2 rashers dry cure bacon, cut into matchsticks
- 1 garlic clove, crushed
- 250g/9oz small onions, peeled
- 400ml/14fl oz bitter beer
- 1 teaspoon brown sugar
- 1/2 teaspoon English mustard

Mix the flour with a scant teaspoon of salt and plenty of black pepper, and turn the beef in it. Heat a frying pan or casserole and cook the bacon gently, adding butter or oil if it doesn't yield much fat. Remove the bacon and brown the meat in the remaining fat. Add the garlic and cook briefly, then the onions, and stir in any remaining flour. Return the bacon to the pan. Add the beer and let it bubble. Stir in the sugar and mustard. Cook very gently at 150°C/300°F/gas mark 2 for 3 hours. The stew is much better left until the next day, when you can lift any solidified fat off the top. Re-heat gently and serve with baked potatoes and glazed carrots.

HAM COOKED IN CIDER

I tested this recipe using mild, succulent gammon from Hindon Farm. The farm was named one of the Soil Association's 'Organic Producers of the Year' in 2003. Hindon is actually just over the border in Somerset but as the ham is cured in traditional Devon fashion it belongs in this chapter. This recipe was orginally recorded by Theodora Fitzgibbon in the 1970s.

Serves 10–12

- 2 1/2 kg/5 1/2 lb Devon-cured ham in a piece
- 1–1 1/2 litre/1 3/4 –2 1/2 pints dry cider
- 1 large onion, peeled and stuck with 6–8 cloves
- 1 tablespoon brown sugar
- 1 lemon
- 2–3 sprigs of fresh parsley and marjoram and a few peppercorns
- 3 tablespoons browned breadcrumbs for coating the meat

Soak the ham overnight in cold water.

Drain, put into a pan in which it fits snugly and add the other ingredients. Bring to the boil, turn the heat down to simmer and cook for 25 minutes per 500g/1lb 2oz. Leave in the stock until almost cold, then remove and allow to drain (keep the stock, providing it is not too salty, as it makes a very good soup). To serve, remove the skin of the ham with a sharp knife and coat the fat with the browned breadcrumbs.

LENTIL AND CARAWAY SOUP

Devised to use stock from cooking ham in cider, this has has a pleasing slightly sour note. Not everyone likes caraway and you may prefer to use cumin instead, which gives a very Middle Eastern flavour.

Serves 6

- 50g/1^3/$_4$oz butter
- 2 medium onions, chopped fairly finely
- 1 teaspoon caraway seeds
- 60g/2oz red lentils
- 1^1/$_2$litres/2^1/$_4$pints stock from the preceding recipe, otherwise use a mixture of chicken stock and dry cider

Melt the butter in a large pan. Add the chopped onions, cover and cook very slowly, stirring occasionally. Eventually they will begin to catch and turn gold. Add the caraway seeds, stir for a moment, then add the lentils and stock. The soup is ready when the lentils are soft (about 30 minutes). Check the seasoning: it is unlikely to need any more salt, especially if using the ham stock.

JUGGED PEAS

To go with all that lovely Devon lamb, this is good even for end-of-season, slightly-past-their-best peas. The herbs transform the dish into something to suit twenty-first- century taste.

Serves 4

- 1kg/2^1/$_4$lb peas in the pod, or 250g/9oz shelled peas
- 25g/1oz butter
- 1 teaspoon granulated sugar
- pinch of salt
- 1–2 tablespoons water
- 2 sprigs of mint
- to finish (optional): 10 sprigs of green coriander, 12 mint leaves and a green chilli, seeded

Put the peas, butter, sugar, salt, water and the sprigs of mint in a small casserole or a pudding basin that will hold them comfortably. Cover with a lid or some foil and place the arrangement in a saucepan of water. Bring this to a gentle boil and simmer for 30 minutes. At the end of this time, the peas should be tender and well flavoured. If a more punchy flavour is desired, chop the coriander, mint leaves and the chilli finely and stir in just before serving.

TURKEY ESCALOPES
WITH LEMON AND THYME

Lemon zest and thyme are tradtional flavourings for stuffings; they work well in this coating for escalopes.

Serves 4

- 2 teaspoons fresh thyme, chopped
- 2 teaspoons lemon zest, finely grated
- salt and pepper
- 120g/4oz fresh white breadcrumbs
- 1 egg, beaten
- 4 turkey escalopes, each weighing 75–100g/3–3 1/2 oz
- butter for frying
- lemon quarters, to serve

Mix the thyme, lemon zest, seasoning and breadcrumbs. Break the egg into a wide bowl and beat to break it up. Dip both sides of each escalope in egg and then coat with the breadcrumb mixture. Heat a little butter in a large frying pan and fry the escalopes gently for 3–4 minutes on each side. You may have to do this in batches – keep the cooked escalopes warm in a low oven. Serve with lemon quarters to squeeze over, and watercress or a green salad.

DEVONSHIRE STEW

Recorded by Florence White in the 1920s, this is not a stew at all, but more like bubble-and-squeak. Good with ham, bacon or eggs.

Serves 4

- 500g/1lb 2oz medium potatoes, not too floury (Desirée work well)
- 2 medium onions
- 250g/9oz cabbage, cut in 2–3 wedges
- 1 teaspoon of salt and plenty of black pepper
- beef dripping or butter

Boil the potatoes, whole and unpeeled, until they are almost done. Peel the onions but leave whole, and boil them until tender. Boil the cabbage briefly and press it in a colander with a plate on top to squeeze out as much water as possible.

When the potatoes are cool enough to handle, peel them and cut into long narrow chip shapes. Shred the onion and cabbage. Mix all together and season.

Heat the dripping or butter in a large frying pan and add the vegetables, stirring until the mixture is nicely browned (it may be necessary to do this in two batches). Serve very hot.

APPLE PANCAKES WITH CIDER SAUCE

Cider-makers sometimes give their products extra flavour by storing them in barrels formerly used for fortified wine or spirits. I used one which had been kept in a rum barrel.

Serves 6

- 2–3 large, well-flavoured apples, peeled, and sliced
- 1 tablespoon water
- 100g/3 $\frac{1}{2}$ oz plain flour
- pinch of salt
- 2 eggs
- 1 tablespoon rum
- 250ml/8 $\frac{1}{2}$ fl oz milk
- 50g/1 $\frac{3}{4}$ oz butter, plus extra for frying
- 50g/1 $\frac{3}{4}$ oz Demerara sugar
- 300ml/10fl oz cider

Put the apple in a saucepan with the water and cook very gently until soft.

Mix the flour and salt with the eggs, then stir in the rum and milk to make a smooth batter. Use this to make 12 thin pancakes. Spread each with a little of the apple purée, roll up and arrange on a heatproof dish. Put in a low oven to warm and crisp a little on the edges.

Melt the butter in a large pan and stir in the sugar. Add the cider, bring to the boil and cook rapidly until the mixture has reduced by at least half and is slightly syrupy. Serve hot with the pancakes.

STEWED PEARS

A delicious variation on pears in red wine, traditionally made at Barnstaple Fair time.

Serves 6

- 6 medium pears, peeled, cored and sliced
- 350g/12oz granulated sugar
- rind and juice of 1 lemon
- 100ml/3 $\frac{1}{2}$ fl oz port
- 3–4 cloves
- 500ml/18fl oz water
- 1 drop of cochineal
- slivered toasted almonds

Put the pears in a pan with the sugar, lemon, port, cloves and enough water to cover. Add a drop of cochineal, if you want them to be really pink. Simmer gently for about 20 minutes or until the pears are tender. Cool and decorate with the almonds. Serve chilled with single cream.

(above) Bracken-covered heathland on The Little Hangman, Devon.
(opposite) 'Beurre d'Aremberg' Pear from *Lindley's British Fruit*, 1846.

TOMATO TARTLETS

I devised this dish with vegetarians in mind, but it works so well everyone else will want some too.

Makes 6

For the pastry
- 80g/3oz well-flavoured Cheddar cheese, grated
- 80g/3oz clotted cream
- 80g/3oz plain flour
- pinch of salt
- 4–5 teaspoons water

For the filling
- 300–400g/10$\frac{1}{2}$–14oz tomatoes, preferably a firm fleshed type (beef tomatoes, if nothing else is available)
- 2 teaspoons English mustard
- 1 tablespoon of fresh basil, torn
- 1 tablespoon of fresh parsley, chopped
- 45g/1$\frac{1}{2}$oz Cheddar cheese, grated
- butter

6 tartlet tins, 9–10cm/3$\frac{1}{2}$–4in in diameter

To make the pastry combine the Cheddar, clotted cream and flour, plus a little salt. Add just enough water to make the mixture into a dough, pressing it together with your fingers. Divide into 6, roll each piece into a circle and use to line the tins. Put the tins in the fridge for 30 minutes to rest the pastry.

Skin the tomatoes, quarter them and discard the seeds and pulp. Slice the flesh neatly. Smear a little of the mustard over the base of each pastry shell. Divide the tomatoes between them, sprinkling in basil and parsley. Divide the remaining Cheddar between the tartlets, and top each with a little knob of butter.

Bake at 220°C/425°F/gas mark 7 for 10–12 minutes. Best eaten warm.

DEVON SCONES

Devon traditions included little bread rolls known as chudleighs, similar to Cornish splits (see page 25), but scones seem to have taken their place.

Makes 16 small fluffy scones

- 240g/8$\frac{1}{2}$oz plain flour, plus extra for dusting
- 1 teaspoon bicarbonate of soda
- 2 teaspoons cream of tartar
- $\frac{1}{2}$teaspoon salt
- 2 teaspoons caster sugar
- 30g/1$\frac{1}{4}$oz butter
- 200ml/7fl oz milk

Mix the flour, bicarbonate of soda, cream of tartar, salt and sugar and sieve together. Rub in the butter. Stir in the milk to make a soft, slightly sticky dough. Flour your hands and a work surface and press the dough together in a coherent mass. Roll out to about 2cm/$\frac{3}{4}$in thick and use a 5$\frac{1}{2}$cm/2$\frac{1}{4}$in round cutter to cut scones. Place on a lightly floured tray and bake at 220°C/425°F/gas mark 7 for 10 minutes.

JUNKET

Simple and good, and much nicer in individual dishes than as one large bowlful.

Serves 6

- 500ml/18fl oz Channel island milk
- 1 heaped dessertspoon caster sugar
- 2 tablespoons brandy
- rennet
- caster sugar, ground cinnamon and clotted cream (optional) to serve

6 ramekin dishes or tumblers

Heat the milk to blood temperature. Dissolve the sugar in it, and stir in the brandy. Consult the instructions for the rennet and stir in the correct amount. *Quickly* divide the mixture between the glasses or tumblers, and leave to set in a cool place.

Just before serving, add a teaspoon of sugar and a dust of cinnamon to the top of each portion. Place a little clotted cream on top for a really rich version.

Lady's bedstraw was used, as the name suggests, to stuff mattresses in the medieval period. However it was also used as a form of rennet.

DEVON WHITEPOT

Originally a whitepot was sausage-like, a distant relative of the hog's puddings still sold in the south-west. By the eighteenth century it was a recipe for a rich, creamy bread and butter pudding, well worth making. Use really good-quality raisins.

Serves 4–6

- $^1/_2$ teaspoon ground ginger
- $^1/_2$ teaspoon ground cinnamon
- 60g/2oz caster sugar
- 30g/1$^1/_4$oz butter, cut into small dice, plus a little extra for greasing
- 100g/3$^1/_2$oz slightly stale white bread, crusts removed, cut in very thin slices
- 60g/2oz dates, stoned and sliced lengthways
- 60g/2oz raisins, stoned if necessary
- 30g/1$^1/_4$oz lemon zest, thinly sliced
- 6 egg yolks, beaten
- 500ml/18fl oz single cream

Use a deep baking dish, such as a 15cm/6in diameter soufflé dish. Butter the base and sides well.

Mix the spices and a little of the sugar and toss the butter cubes in it. Then build up the pudding in the dish, starting with a layer of bread. Scatter half the butter cubes, dates, raisins and lemon zest over, add another layer of bread, the rest of the butter and fruit, and finish with a neatly arranged layer of bread.

Beat the egg yolks, cream and the rest of the sugar together, and pour over the pudding; the bread should absorb the mixture, although you may have to press it down a little in the process.

Bake at 170°C/325°F/gas mark 3 for 30–40 minutes, until the custard is just set and the top golden brown. Serve hot.

The cider apple press at Buckland Abbey, Devon.

A vew of the Maldon Hills, Devon.

Also known as brandysnaps, these thin crisp biscuits were associated with several other fairs in southern England. Eat alone, fill with whipped cream, or serve with creamy desserts.

Makes 15

- 50g/1¹/₂ oz butter
- 50g/1¹/₂ oz Demerara sugar
- 50g/1¹/₂ oz golden syrup
- 50g/1¹/₂ oz plain flour
- ¹/₂ teaspoon ground ginger
- 1 teaspoon lemon juice
- 1–2 teaspoons brandy

Put the butter, sugar and syrup in a pan and melt over a low heat. When liquid, stir in the flour, ginger, lemon juice and brandy.

Drop teaspoons of the mixture, widely spaced – the biscuits spread as they cook – on non-stick baking trays or trays lined with baking paper. Cook at 190°C/375°F/gas mark 5 for about 5 minutes. Remove from the oven, leave on the trays to cool for a minute, then lift each biscuit with a palette knife and wrap round the handle of a wooden spoon. If the biscuits cool too much, they can be returned to the oven for a moment to soften; or they may be left flat. When fully cooled, store in an airtight container.

Adding some redcurrant juice to the strawberries produces a better set and intensifies the flavour without being too obvious.

- 500g/1lb 2oz redcurrants
- 500g/1lb 2oz strawberries
- 500g/1lb 2oz granulated sugar

Begin the day before by placing the redcurrants in a pan; put the lid on and cook over a very gentle heat until they have collapsed and yielded all their juice. Remove from the heat and pour the fruit into a jelly bag with a bowl underneath to catch the juice. There should be about 200ml/7fl oz.

The next day, hull the strawberries, remove any bad bits, and rinse them; halve or quarter large ones. Place in a pan with the sugar and the redcurrant juice, and heat gently, stirring to dissolve the sugar. Once this is done, bring to the boil and cook for about 15–20 minutes, then test a drop on a chilled saucer for setting. If the jam crinkles when lightly pushed with a finger, it's set. When the setting point is reached, pour into warm, sterilised jars and seal immediately.

(above) 'Duchesna Indica' or Indian Mock Strawberry from the garden at Greenway, Devon.

LALLAH'S CHUTNEY

Who Lallah was is unrecorded, but her chutney recipe lives on. Like most chutneys, it is better matured for a few weeks before eating.

- 500ml/18fl oz malt vinegar
- 40g/1 1/2 oz salt
- 250g/9oz granulated sugar
- 1kg/2 1/4 lb large apples, peeled and sliced
- 70g/2 1/2 oz preserved ginger in syrup, drained and sliced
- 60g/2oz sultanas
- 25g/1oz fresh hot chillies, seeded and chopped
- 1 tablespoon mustard powder
- 1 shallot, chopped
- 1 medium onion, sliced

Pour the vinegar over the salt and sugar, then place in a large pan with all other ingredients. Simmer gently for three hours until tender. Pot in warmed, sterilised jars.

MARROW, TOMATO AND DATE CHUTNEY

Sara Paston-Williams remarks that this is good for using up gluts and excellent with beef burgers.

- 1.35kg/3lb marrow
- 80g/3oz salt
- 900g/2lb red tomatoes, skinned and chopped
- 225g/8oz onions, peeled and chopped
- 350g/12oz cooking apples, peeled, cored and sliced
- 600ml/1 pint distilled malt vinegar
- 225g/8oz cooking dates, stoned and chopped
- 450g/1lb soft light brown sugar
- 1 tablespoon mustard seeds
- 2 tablespoons ground ginger
- 2 teaspoons ground allspice

Peel the marrow, cut in half, remove and discard the seeds. Dice the flesh into 1cm/ 1/2 in cubes and layer these in a bowl with the salt. Cover and leave for 24 hours.

Next day, rinse the salted marrow under cold running water and drain well. Put the tomatoes, onions and apples in a large preserving pan. Add the vinegar, stir well, then bring to the boil. Reduce the heat and cook gently for 30 minutes. Add the dates, sugar and spices, followed by the marrow. Stir well and bring back to the boil. Reduce the heat and simmer for 1 1/2 –2 hours until thick, stirring occasionally to prevent sticking. Pour into warm, sterilised jars and store for 2–3 months before eating.

(above) Sheepdogs 'holding' the sheep at Morte Point, Devon.

THE MARCHES

The Marches is the land along the boundary
between England and Wales, running from
the Bristol Channel northwards up the Wye
Valley, taking in Hereford and Leominster, onwards past
Shrewsbury and following the course of the River Dee to
Chester. The concept is as much historical as geographical.
Once an important frontier, the area is littered with
markers such as Offa's Dyke, which runs in a series of dots
and dashes between the estuaries of the Severn and Dee,
and medieval castles in various states of repair, from the

splendour of Chirk to the ruinous Skenfrith. The political
boundary follows a geographical one, for here the generally
flat western extremity of the English Midlands meets the
Welsh mountains. The hills are never far away, getting
higher to the west. In the southernmost part, the River Wye
loops through them in a deep, enclosed gorge, and they
close in around the pretty town of Ludlow. The rocky
fingers of the Long Mynd and Wenlock Edge reach north-
east towards Shrewsbury and the Cheshire plain. To the
east, the scenery is not entirely level; the grassy, undulating

(previous page) Misty woodland in the Clent Hills, Worcestershire.
(above) Skenfrith Castle in Monmouthshire on the border with Wales.

ridge of the Malverns, the sharp cone of the Wrekin and the Peckforton Hills south of Chester add variety to this flatter landscape.

However much this area may have been fought over in the past, it is now tranquil and the lower parts are domesticated and very appealing. It is a countryside of mixed farming, with pasture and meadow and some cultivated land, and, in the southern part at least, orchards. It feels timeless and deeply rural.

In the northern part of the Marches, Shropshire and Cheshire have been dairy counties for centuries. The area has a mild, damp climate which produces excellent pasture; the salt deposits which lie deep below the Cheshire plain are said to give a distinctive flavour to the milk of cattle grazed here and, in turn, to contribute to the excellence of true Cheshire cheese. The importance of dairying is acknowledged in the form of the Nantwich Cheese Show at which British cheeses in all their variety are displayed. Cattle are important over much of the rest of the Marches, either for milk or beef. Of the latter, Herefords with their copper flanks and white heads were developed in the late eighteenth and early nineteenth century in the county from which they take their name. Beef cattle and sheep become increasingly important in the western part of the Marches as the hills become higher and the climate more challenging. The area also developed its own native sheep breed, named after the little town of Clun that is buried in the hills close to the Welsh border. Another source of meat, represented on National Trust land in

this area, are deer. They were once the exclusive preserve of the aristocracy, including the Marcher lords whose ruined castles still dominate some of the towns.

Herefordshire, protected from the worst of the rain by the Black Mountains to the west, provides some especially pleasing landscapes of half-timbered buildings, as seen at Cwmmau Farmhouse, scattered among orchards. Apples and pears were both grown for dessert fruit, cooking and for drinks. Cider is as important here as it is in the South-west, and the area is a centre of perry making, a pleasant drink when not over-industrialised. The county also grows a major part of the British blackcurrant crop, used both for dessert and cordials, and hops are grown in the Teme valley. It is stretching things to say that the Marches include the Vale of Evesham, on the eastern side of the Severn, but the tradition of fruit growing continues here with apples, pears and plums in Worcestershire. Asparagus was a famous crop of this area, but is sadly less important than it used to be. Other fruit crops of local importance include damsons in Shropshire, and gooseberries (which extends beyond jam to the cut-throat competitions of the Cheshire gooseberry shows).

The general cookery tradition echoes that of England as a whole, and local specialities recorded in the past seem a little neglected. Shrewsbury Cakes, so well-known in the seventeenth century that Congreve could say someone was 'as short as a Shrewsbury cake', seem to have been forgotten in the town.

(top) The traditional half-timbered architecture of Lower Brockhampton in Worcestershire.

Several National Trust estates on the counties bordering Wales produce venison. At Attingham Park, a herd of fallow deer graces Humphry Repton's landscape, and their meat is available in limited quantities through the winter months. It responds well to *boeuf a laBourguignon* treatment. This is not a traditional British farmhouse recipe, but it is very good. Although it takes a relatively long time to cook, I think it tastes as good or better made in advance and re-heated.

Serves 6–8

- 900g/2lb stewing venison, cut in slices 8 x 8cm (3 $\frac{1}{4}$ x 3 $\frac{1}{4}$ in) and $\frac{1}{2}$ cm ($\frac{1}{4}$ in) thick
- 1 onion, sliced
- 1 garlic clove, crushed
- 4–6 juniper berries, bruised
- 100ml/3 $\frac{1}{2}$ fl oz red wine
- olive oil
- salt and pepper
- 25g/1oz beef dripping
- 4 rashers unsmoked bacon, cut in strips
- 250g/9oz button mushrooms, washed, trimmed and sliced
- 1 tablespoon plain flour
- 300ml/10fl oz beef stock
- bouquet garni of parsley, thyme, marjoram, a bay leaf and a strip of orange peel

Put the venison, onion, garlic, juniper berries, wine and a tablespoon of olive oil in a bowl, plus a scant teaspoon salt and a generous grind of pepper. Cover and leave to marinate overnight.

The next day, tip the meat into a sieve over a bowl and allow to drain, reserving the marinade. Melt the dripping (or use a little more olive oil) in a heavy casserole and add the bacon. Cook gently and remove when it shows signs of crisping. Cook the mushrooms in the same fat until soft. Lift out with a slotted spoon and put aside with the bacon.

Toss the drained meat (don't worry too much about disentangling the onion) in the flour and brown it in the fat. Add the marinade and stir well, then pour in the stock, stirring while the mixture comes to the boil. Put the bouquet garni in among the meat, cover, and transfer to a low oven, 140–150°C/275–300°F/gas mark 1–2 for about 3 hours. Towards the end of cooking, stir in the bacon and mushrooms and check the seasoning. Serve with jacket potatoes or some *parpadelle*, tossed with a little butter and chopped parsley.

Fallow deer on the south lawn at Dunham Massey, Cheshire.

VENISON SAUCE

A little care is needed when roasting venison because the meat tends to dry out. Use haunch or saddle. It is worth taking the trouble to lard it (using a special larding needle to insert small pieces of pork back fat over the surface of the meat at regular intervals). Cook for 15-20 minutes per 500g/1lb 2oz at 200°C/400°F/gas mark 6. Baste frequently and allow it to rest before carving. Serve it with this old-fashioned but good late nineteenth-century sauce, derived from the haute cuisine tradition.

- 50g/1³/₄oz butter
- ¹/₂ large onion, sliced
- 2 rashers lean unsmoked bacon, chopped
- 1 stick celery, chopped
- 2 cloves
- 6 peppercorns
- 2–3 large sprigs of thyme
- 1 bayleaf
- 1 dessertspoon plain flour
- 500ml/18fl oz stock, made either from the deer bones or from beef
- 1 dessertspoon redcurrant jelly
- 100ml/3¹/₂fl oz red wine
- salt

Melt the butter in a large frying pan and add the onion, bacon, celery, cloves, peppercorns, thyme and the bayleaf. Fry briskly, stirring frequently, until the vegetables are golden brown. Stir in the flour, then the stock and simmer for an hour.

Strain the contents of the pan into a bowl, pressing to extract as much flavour as possible. Return the liquid to the pan and add the redcurrant jelly. In a separate pan, boil the wine until it is reduced to about 2 tablespoons liquid, and stir into the sauce. Cook gently for a few minutes, check the seasoning and serve very hot with a roast of venison.

ASPARAGUS TARTLETS

Asparagus is grown all over the country, but the Vale of Evesham was famous for this crop.

Makes 18

- 500g/1lb 2oz asparagus
- 25g/1oz butter, plus a little extra
- salt and pepper
- 2 egg yolks
- 1 quantity shortcrust pastry, (see page 13)

Wash and trim the asparagus stems, cutting off the hard ends of the stalks. Place the asparagus in a pan and just cover with water. Simmer until the stems are tender. Drain and cut the tips off and reserve. Put the rest in a processor or blender and reduce to a purée. Beat in the butter and season with salt and pepper. Stir in the egg yolks.

Roll the pastry thinly and use to line patty pans. Divide the asparagus mixture between them. Decorate with the reserved tips and dot with butter. Bake at 190°C/375°F/gas mark 5 for about 15 minutes. Serve warm.

GOOSEBERRY JELLY

Most gooseberries produce a russet-coloured jam or jelly. Allegedly, this method gives a green jelly, but it depends on your gooseberries and possibly their stage of ripeness. Leveller is one variety in which the juice remains green but even this came out reddish for me, perhaps because they were too ripe. It still tastes good, though.

- 900g/2lb gooseberries, topped, tailed and washed
- 300ml/10fl oz water
- granulated sugar (see method for quantity)

Put the berries in a pan with the water. Cook gently until they collapse. Place in a jelly bag and allow to drip overnight. The next day, measure the quantity of juice, and allow 450g/1lb sugar per 600ml/20fl oz of juice. Put the sugar in an ovenproof dish and place it in a warm oven to heat through. Put the juice in a pan and bring to the boil, and then cook gently for about 10 minutes. Add the hot sugar, stir to dissolve, and bring to the boil. Start testing for setting point fairly soon afterwards (see page 51). Skim and pot in warm, sterilised jars.

'Compton's Sheba Queen' Gooseberry from *Lindley's British Fruits*, 1846.

OLDBURY GOOSEBERRY PIES

These pies are made with a hot-water crust and a hand-raised shell. The recipe and method is local to Oldbury-on-Severn, where the pies are still made for summer fêtes and fund-raising events. Traditionally, the edges are nipped up into twenty-one little points, and the pies themselves full of juice. Make the pies up the day before you cook them for the best results.

Makes 8

- 500g/1lb 2oz plain flour
- 120g/4oz butter
- 120g/4oz lard
- 5 tablespoons boiling water
- 750g/1lb 10oz small green gooseberries
- 250–325g/9–11oz Demerara sugar

Put the flour in a bowl. Cut the butter and lard into small dice, make a well in the centre of the flour and place the fat in it. Pour the boiling water over and rapidly mix until you have a warm, malleable dough. Divide into 8 pieces and work with one piece at a time; keep the remainder covered with a cloth, in a warm place. Take the piece of dough, cut away a quarter to make a lid, and roll the rest out into a circle slightly smaller than a saucer. Make the tart cases by turning the edges up by 2cm/³⁄₄in all round, pinching the pastry so that it stands up. Fill with some of the gooseberries and a fairly liberal amount of sugar. Roll the smaller piece of pastry into a circle big enough for a lid, brush with water and use it to cover the berries and sugar, pinching the edges together all round. Repeat with the other pieces of pastry.

Place on baking trays and leave overnight in a cool place for the pastry to set. Bake at 200–220°C/400–425°F/gas mark 6–7 for 25–30 minutes. Serve tepid or allow to cool. I've never managed to make them without some juice escaping, but they still taste good.

The Long Mynd in Shropshire offers stunning views and is a Site of Special Scientific Interest.

BLACKCURRANT LIQUEUR

Blackcurrants became a field crop in Herefordshire for manufacturing soft drinks. This in an alcoholic version for grown ups.

- 300ml/ 1/2 pint gin
- 350g/12oz blackcurrants
- 175g/6oz sugar
- 2 cloves

Steep all the ingredients together for six weeks, strain and bottle. Excellent.

ELDERFLOWER CORDIAL

Until about 1990, if you wanted elderflower cordial you had to make it. I still think home-made cordial tastes better than the commercial versions, but the elderflowers must be gathered on a dry day and used immediately or they develop an unpleasant smell.

- 20 heads elderflower in full blossom
- 1.6kg/4lb granulated sugar
- 1.6 litres/2 1/2 pints water, boiled and cooled
- 60g/2oz tartaric acid
- 2 whole lemons, sliced
- 2 whole oranges, sliced

Put all the ingredients in a large pan and stir periodically for 24 hours. Strain and pour into sterilised bottles. For use, dilute to taste.

GOOSEBERRIES WITH ELDERFLOWER ZABAGLIONE

I don't think gooseberry fool (cooked, crushed berries, custard and whipped cream) can be improved on, but sometimes one might want a change. Make the purée in advance. The zabaglione is a last-minute task.

Serves 4

- 300g/10 oz gooseberries
- 4 egg yolks
- 4 tablespoons granulated sugar
- 4 tablespoons elderflower cordial
- 1 tablespoon vodka (optional)

Put the gooseberries in a pan with just enough water to cover the base. Cook gently until soft, then sieve. Chill the purée.

Just before serving, divide the purée between four shallow dishes. Put the egg yolks and the sugar in a bowl and beat with a whisk until pale yellow. Add the cordial and vodka. Put the bowl over a pan of simmering water (don't let it touch the water, or it will curdle) and keep beating until thick and foamy. Divide this between the dishes and serve immediately, perhaps with some little almond biscuits.

Elderflowers in full bloom.

Dutch Mignonne Apple from *Lindley's British Fruit,* 1846.

Recorded in the 1930s, an unusual and extremely good variation of cheese on toast.

Serves 4

- 4–8 rashers bacon (depending on size of rashers and appetites)
- 4 slices white bread
- 150g/5 ¹/₂ oz Cheshire cheese, sliced
- 2 apples peeled, cored and sliced
- pepper
- a little sugar

Fry the bacon. When cooked, put to the side and fry the bread in the bacon fat. Remove, cover with the sliced cheese and put under the grill to cook gently. Add the apple slices to the remaining bacon fat and fry gently, turning once or twice. When the cheese has melted, divide the bacon between the toasts and top with the apple slices. Dust the apple with a suspicion of sugar and grind a little pepper over everything.

For a lower-fat version, grill the bacon and toast the bread.

Recipes for these changed over the years from thick, delicately spiced shortcakes to biscuits with currants in them. This is based on a recipe in a manuscript of 1847, with the addition of flavours that recall eighteenth-century recipes.

Makes 40

- 250g/9oz caster sugar
- 250g/9oz softened butter
- 375g/13oz plain flour
- ¹/₂ teaspoon cinnamon
- ¹/₂ teaspoon nutmeg
- 1 egg yolk
- 1 tablespoon sherry
- 1 tablespoon rosewater (or use extra sherry)
- ¹/₄ teaspoon salt
- caraway seeds (optional)

Mix the sugar and butter, stirring until well amalgamated and soft. Add the flour and spices, the egg yolk and the sherry and rosewater. Mix thoroughly. A little extra sherry or rosewater may be needed to produce a coherent pastry, but try not to let it become sticky. Allow the mixture to rest for half an hour.

Roll out to 5mm/¹/₄ in thick and cut in rounds. Place on baking trays and bake at 170°C/325°F/gas mark 3 for about 15 minutes; try not to let the cakes brown.

Transfer the biscuits to a wire rack; they will crisp up as they cool. Store in an airtight container.

The unique rock houses at Kinver Edge, Staffordshire. The houses look like conventional houses but are built into the sandstone rock.

Espaliered 'Reinette' pears at Westbury Court Garden, Gloucestershire.

PEAR AND GINGER JAM

A tree of hard cooking pears was often planted next to a farmhouse, for jams and pickles.

- 1kg/2 1/4 lb cooking pears, peeled, cored and chopped
- 10g/ 1/4 oz ginger root, shredded
- 450ml/ 3/4 pint water
- zest and juice of 1 lemon
- 800g/1lb 11oz granulated sugar

Put the pears, ginger and water in a pan and add the juice and zest of the lemon. Stew gently until the pear is soft. Measure the contents of the pan and add 500g/1lb 2oz sugar per 500ml/18fl oz pear mixture. Boil until setting point is reached (see page 51) and pot in warm, sterile jars.

PICKLED PEARS

To eat with cold meat.

- 2kg/4 1/2 lb hard pears, peeled, halved and cored (use under-ripe eating pears if no cooking pears are available)
- lemon juice
- 1kg/2 1/4 lb sugar
- 3 cloves
- 200ml/7fl oz distilled malt vinegar

Drop the prepared pears into a bowl of water with a squeeze of lemon to prevent browning. Put the sugar, cloves and vinegar in a large pan and stir well. Add the pears and bring to the boil. Cover and simmer very gently until tender. Time depends on the pear variety; under-ripe Williams take about 1 1/2 hours, but hard cooking pears may take much longer. Pot the pears and syrup in warm, sterilised jars and cover with parchment paper.

GARDEN OF ENGLAND

As the term 'garden of England' suggests, growing fruit and vegetables has been important here for centuries, and in places the landscape does have a minutely tended feel. Not that it was ever entirely 'garden'. The south coast – Hampshire, Sussex and Kent – includes the high, bare chalk hills of the South Downs which run from Winchester and end abruptly at Beachy Head almost 100 miles to the east. To the south, the chalk re-appears as the Isle of Wight. The northern edge of these counties is marked by the dramatic ridge of the North Downs, which meet the sea at Dover. The landscape between the two ranges of hills is sometimes flat clay-filled valleys, at other times undulating and hilly, and by no means all cultivated. To the west of London chalk rolls through Salisbury Plain and the Marlborough Downs, and also appears to the north in the Chilterns.

The South Downs were famous in the past for grazing huge flocks of sheep, leading to a characteristic close-cropped grass sward. In recent years, the Downs have changed, with some land being ploughed and some reverting to scrub as the number of grazing sheep has diminished. Sheep-grazing was also important on the Levels of Pevensey and Romney Marsh. Traditional animal breeds in the area include Romneys and various breeds of downland sheep; Southdowns were famous in the nineteenth century as providers of the mutton so important to the Victorian kitchen. Poultry-rearing was of great consequence in Sussex and Surrey up until the Second World War.

Inland, perhaps the strongest distinguishing feature of much of the land between the Downs is the presence of trees, although the gale of 1987 felled many of the older ones. The word 'forest', from the New Forest on the western edge of Hampshire through to Lyminge Forest in east Kent, actually indicates trees interspersed with areas of heath. Being in the south does not mean a consistently warmer, easier climate, and although summers are hotter and drier than in much of Britain, the eastern part of Kent tends to catch cold easterly winds and snow in winter.

The constraints of modern agriculture and competition from abroad have possibly made the area less of a garden than it once was. Watercress is a special crop, grown in the clear water of springs which emerge at the junction of chalk and clay strata; Hampshire is the principal watercress-growing county in the area. Some farmers have experimented with more novel crops, such as garlic

(previous page) Bales of hay near Chyngton Farm, East Sussex with the spectacular Seven Sisters cliffs in the background.

(above)The Oast Houses at Outridge Farm, Kent.

on the Isle of Wight and, in the sheltered environment of a former walled garden at Slindon near Arundel, pumpkins and squashes. Fruit-growing gives a special character to the high Weald of Kent and Sussex, and is also important in an area to the north-west of London. England's favourite apple, the Cox's Orange Pippin, does well in this climate. Plums and cherries also grow happily, and Kent has a few commercial producers of hazelnuts. Kent's other major crop, hops, is not as important as it used to be, but evidence remains in the oast houses, with their pyramidal roofs and white air vents essential for hop-drying. Soft fruit is also grown, and Hampshire is noted for its early strawberries.

The food of much of south-east England has largely lost any special character it may have had under the onslaught of metropolitan influence. Until the Second World War, a distinguishing feature seems to have been the use of suet crust in savoury and sweet puddings. Just as it is said that a Cornishwoman will put anything in a pasty, so it seems that housewives from the south-east made puddings. In poor households they might be plain, served with gravy or syrup as rib-sticking food for large and hungry families; in better-off establishments they included meat, sometimes game, or fruit. Home-baking was less important than in some areas, due partly to an eighteenth- and nineteenth-century shortage of fuel for wood-fired ovens – some of the woodland cover of this area was planted relatively recently. However, the south-east shared the general British tradition of the cottage pig, making hams, bacon, sausages and 'flead cake', a local variation of the lardy cake.

GARDEN OF ENGLAND

(top) Poppies carpeting a dip in a field in Alfriston, East Sussex.
(bottom) Sheep crossing a hollow on Fulking Escarpment, West Sussex.

WOOD-PIGEON STEW

Wood-pigeons gorge on grain crops. Unusually for game, they are available all year round and make a good late-summer ragout. This recipe originally used whole birds - if you want to do this, braise them gently for about an hour. You can ask your butcher to prepare the birds for you - make sure you retain the carcasses for making stock.

Serves 4

- 4 oven-ready wood-pigeons, skinned and breasts removed
- 25g/1oz butter
- 100g/3 1/2 oz fatty bacon, cut in strips
- 200g/7oz button mushrooms, sliced
- plain flour, for dusting
- 400ml/14fl oz chicken, beef or game stock
- 2 tablespoons mushroom ketchup
- 200–250g/6–9oz shelled peas
- salt, pepper and lemon juice

Melt the butter in a casserole which can be used on the hob and add the bacon and mushrooms. Cook gently together until the bacon is transparent and has yielded much of its fat. Remove the bacon and mushrooms with a slotted spoon. Dust the pigeon breasts with flour and fry gently in the bacon fat until brown on both sides, then put to one side with the bacon and mushrooms. Add a little more flour to the remaining fat and stir to make a roux. Stir in the stock to make a smooth sauce and add the mushroom ketchup. Put the bacon and mushrooms back in the sauce and add the peas, frozen ones work as well as fresh. Place the pigeon breasts on top. Stew gently on the top of the stove for about 25 minutes, turning the pigeon breasts occasionally – they should be almost cooked, with a trace of pink at the centre. Taste the sauce and add salt, pepper and lemon juice to taste. Allow to rest for 5 minutes and serve with new potatoes.

DEVILLED CHICKEN

Surrey and Sussex were famous for chickens and capons up until the Second World War; they were expensive and considered a treat. 'Devilling' poultry or game in a spicy sauce was popular at the turn of the twentieth century.

Serves 4–6

- 1 chicken, jointed
- salt
- 300ml/10fl oz single cream
- 1 tablespoon Madras curry powder
- 1 tablespoon dry mustard powder

Season the chicken with salt and cook under a hot grill, turning frequently, until the juices run clear when the thickest part is pierced with a skewer. The chicken can be baked, but is not as succulent.

Mix the cream, curry powder and mustard in a frying pan. Add the pieces of chicken and any meaty juices from the grill pan. Heat gently; the mixture will thicken as it comes to the boil.

Serve with plain boiled rice.

The pond at Woodhouse Farm, an organic farm on the Buscot Estate, Oxfordshire.

Savoury pudding fillings recorded in Kent and Sussex include mutton and oysters, partridges, and a chicken and ham version from Staplehurst in Kent. They should really be made by putting uncooked meat into the crust and boiling or steaming for several hours, and belong to the days of iron monster ranges, always hot and demanding the constant presence of the farmer's wife or a servant to make sure they weren't boiling dry. This version has been adapted to cut the steaming time.

Serves 4–6

- 1 chicken, skinned and boned except for the wing joints, cut into large pieces
- plain flour to coat
- butter for frying
- 400ml/14fl oz good chicken stock
- salt and pepper
- 1 tablespoon fresh, chopped tarragon
- 1 tablespoon fresh, chopped parsley
- 100g/3 1/2 oz well-flavoured cooked ham, cut in strips
- 100g/3 1/2 oz button mushrooms, wiped and chopped

For the suet crust
- 100g/3 1/2 oz fresh white breadcrumbs
- 200g/7oz self-raising flour
- 1/2 teaspoon salt
- 1 teaspoon lemon zest
- 120g/4oz suet
- water to mix

A 1.2-litre/2-pint pudding basin and a saucepan large enough to hold it and a quantity of boiling water.

Flour the chicken. Melt the butter in a large frying pan and add the chicken pieces. Fry gently, turning from time to time, until golden brown on all sides. Add the stock, cover and simmer gently for 40 minutes, then allow to cool slightly. Season rather highly with salt and add the pepper, tarragon and parsley.

Meanwhile, make the suet pastry by combining the breadcrumbs, flour, salt, lemon zest and suet. Add enough water to make a coherent dough and line the basin (see page 13), reserving a quarter of the pastry to form the lid. Lift the chicken out of the cooking liquid and layer it, the ham and the mushrooms in the lined basin. Pour the cooking liquid over the meat.

Roll the reserved pastry into a round to fit the top of the pudding. Seal the edges neatly. Take a large double piece of tin foil or greaseproof paper, make a generous pleat in the middle and cover the top of the basin with it, remembering that the pudding will expand a little as it cooks. Tie a piece of string round the top of the basin to hold the tin foil in place, and take the string across the top of the basin to make a handle.

Lower the covered pudding into boiling water and cook steadily for 1 1/2 hours, adding more boiling water if it shows signs of boiling dry. Tie a napkin round the basin and serve.

A farmer feeding free-range hens at Osterley Park, London.

STEAK AND KIDNEY PIE OR PUDDING

Another salute to the south-eastern tradition of puddings. Using raw partridges preserves their delicious flavour, but the pudding needs several hours steaming.

Mr Bristow, who farms near Redhill on the southern slopes of the North Downs, produces superb-quality lamb and Aberdeen Angus beef. Try it in this steak and kidney mixture, good in either a pie or a pudding.

Serves 4

- 2 partridges
- 350g/12oz self-raising flour, plus extra for dusting
- 150g/5^1/$_2$oz suet
- 150g/5^1/$_2$oz rump steak, thinly sliced
- 100g/3^1/$_2$oz mushrooms, sliced
- salt and pepper
- 1 tablespoon chopped, fresh parsley
- 1 tablespoon chopped, fresh thyme
- 100ml/3^1/$_2$fl oz red wine

A 1.2- litre/2- pint pudding basin

Firstly skin and joint the partridges, or ask your butcher to do it for you. Use the carcasses with a bouquet garni, an onion and a carrot to make a little stock.

To make the pudding combine the flour, suet and a pinch of salt, and add enough water to make a coherent dough. Use this to line the pudding basin (see page 13). Line the bottom of the crust with the sliced steak and then put in the partridge joints and sliced mushrooms in layers, sprinkling salt, pepper and chopped herbs in between. Mix the wine with stock and pour over the filling. Cover the pudding with pastry and place tin foil or greaseproof paper over the top of the basin. Tie well and cook for at least 3 hours.

Serves 4–6

- 40g/1^1/$_2$oz dripping
- 1 large onion, chopped
- 3 tablespoons plain flour
- salt and pepper
- 500g/1lb 2oz stewing beef, trimmed and cut in 2cm/1in cubes
- 150–200g/5^1/$_2$–7oz ox kidney, trimmed and cut in 1cm/^{1}/$_2$in cubes
- 400ml/14fl oz beef stock
- 1 bay leaf
- ^{1}/$_2$teaspoon ground allspice
- Worcestershire sauce

A 1.2-litre/2-pint pudding basin or a pie dish

Melt a little of the dripping in a large pan and cook the onion gently for about 30 minutes until soft. Remove to a casserole.

Mix 2 tablespoons of flour with half a teaspoon of salt and some pepper, toss the beef and kidney in it. Add the rest of the dripping to the frying pan and brown the meat, in batches if necessary, transferring to the casserole when done. Sprinkle another tablespoon or so of flour into the frying pan to take up any remaining fat and gradually stir in the beef stock, scraping the base of the pan to incorporate all the juices from cooking the meat. It doesn't matter if the mixture includes a few lumps at this stage. Bring to the boil and cook for a few minutes, then pour over the meat. Add the bay leaf, allspice and a splash of Worcestershire sauce. Cover, transfer to the oven and cook at, 170°C/325°F/gas mark 3 for 2 hours. At the end, taste and add more seasoning if necessary.

Allow to cool and then use either in a pudding (use the crust for Partridge Pudding left, and steam for 1^1/$_2$ hours) or in a pie, covered with puff pastry.

CARAMELISED BAKED PUMPKIN

Mr Upton, began gardening at Slindon on the south coast in the 1950s. As he couldn't interest anyone in the traditional apple varieties growing there, he began cultivating pumpkins and squashes instead. This recipe works well with any variety.

Serves 4–6 as a vegetable dish to accompany meat

- 1kg/2¼lb pumpkin, peeled, de-seeded and stringy centre removed
- 25g/1oz butter
- salt and freshly ground black pepper
- 2 tablespoons Demerara sugar

Cut the pumpkin into rough cubes. Melt the butter in a shallow ovenproof dish. Add the pumpkin and turn it in the butter so that it is well coated. Sprinkle with salt, pepper and the sugar. Bake at 250°C/475°F/gas mark 9 for 15 minutes, reducing the heat to 220°C/425°F/gas mark 7 for a further 10 minutes, or until the pumpkin is tender. Serve immediately.

Squash ripening in the sun; 'Turk's Head" (top) and 'Mini Turban' (bottom).

PUMPKIN CREAM

A variation on a marrow recipe used by my mother.

- 500g/1lb 2oz pumpkin, peeled and seeded weight
- 500g/1lb 2oz granulated sugar
- 60g/2oz butter
- zest of ½ orange
- juice and zest of 1 lemon

Cube the pumpkin and put in a large saucepan. Add enough water to cover the base of the pan and stew gently until the pumpkin is soft and can be crushed. Add a little more water if necessary, and stir to make sure it doesn't catch. Once the pumpkin has collapsed, add the sugar, butter, orange and lemon zest and the lemon juice. Cook rapidly until the mixture is thick – about 20 minutes. Pot in hot, sterilised jars. Eat within 6 weeks.

WATERCRESS SAUCE FOR TROUT OR SALMON

Layers of chalk and clay in a landscape give springs of pure water. Clean water is the best environment for growing watercress. If you're lucky, it also means good streams for trout fishing.

- 1 bunch watercress
- 300ml/10fl oz water or fish stock
- 25g/1oz butter
- 25g/1oz plain flour
- 1 tablespoon double cream
- salt, pepper, lemon juice

Strip the leaves from the cress and reserve. Chop the stalks and cook gently in the water or stock until just soft. Make a roux with the butter and flour, and strain in the cooking liquid (discard the cress stems). Cook gently, stirring constantly, until the sauce thickens. Stir in the cream and adjust the seasoning, adding a squeeze of lemon juice to taste. Finally, add the reserved cress leaves and serve immediately with fish or eggs.

KIDNEYS IN ONIONS

A dish popular on the south coast and Isle of Wight. Well-flavoured beef stock is essential.

Serves 4

- 4 large onions
- 4 sheep's kidneys
- salt, ground allspice
- chopped parsley
- 4 bay leaves
- 4 cloves
- 450ml/14fl oz beef stock
- 50ml/2fl oz rum

Peel the onions, slicing off the root end so they will stand level, and trimming any papery bits from the stem end. Cut a 'lid' off the top of each one and keep on one side. Hollow out the top of each onion so that a kidney will fit neatly. Season the insides with a little salt, a dust of allspice and a little chopped parsley. Nestle the kidneys into the hollows, put the lids on and put a bay leaf on top of each onion, spearing it in place with a clove. Put the onions in a heavy pan or casserole in which they fit neatly and add the stock. Put the lid on, bring to the boil, and then simmer very gently for $1^1/_2$ hours. Add the rum and simmer another 30 minutes, allowing the stock to reduce a little. Taste the stock and adjust the seasoning. Serve in soup bowls, with a spoon and fork for eating the dish, and some good bread to mop up the liquid.

Watercress in full flower.

The Kent version of fine white bread rolls.

Makes 12

- 1 teaspoon granulated sugar
- 1 dessertspoon dried yeast
- 300ml/10fl oz milk, hand-hot
- ½ teaspoon salt
- 500g/1lb 2oz strong plain flour
- 30g/1¼oz lard

Add the sugar and yeast to the warm milk and set aside for a few minutes until it forms a frothy head. Mix the salt into the flour and rub in the lard. Stir in the yeast mixture and make up into a dough, adding a little water if necessary. Knead for 10 minutes, then put the dough in an oiled bowl and cover with a damp cloth. Allow to rise in a warm place until doubled in size, for about 1 hour.

Knock back and divide into 12 pieces. Roll each one out into an oval about 13cm/5in long. Place on greased baking trays and make a hole in the centre of each oval. Flour well and prove until well risen. Bake in a hot oven, 220°C/425°F/gas mark 7 for 15–20 minutes. Wrap in a warm cloth to preserve the soft crust as they cool.

SPICED TOMATO JELLY

The original recipe, from *The Country Housewife's Handbook* (Kent W.I.), was very lightly spiced, in keeping with the tastes of the mid-twentieth century. Add extra flavour at the end for something more robust. Excellent with cheese and cold meats.

- 1½kg/3lb 5oz ripe tomatoes
- 6 cloves
- ½ stick cinnamon
- 500g/1lb 2oz preserving sugar (with added pectin, specially for jam-making)
- 1kg/2¼lb granulated sugar
- 850ml/1¼pints water
- 150ml/5fl oz white wine vinegar
- 2 red chillies, seeds and strings removed, cut into tiny dice
- 3 garlic cloves, peeled and sliced into paper-thin rounds
- 3cm/1¼in ginger root, peeled and finely shredded

Chop the tomatoes and put in a large pan. Cook gently with the spices until soft. Sieve. Add the sugar and vinegar and bring to the boil. Add the chillies, garlic and ginger and cook gently until setting point is reached. Pot in warm sterilised jars.

SALAD SAUCE

An old-fashioned English salad dressing. Delicious with freshly gathered, crisp, green lettuce hearts.

- 2 hard boiled egg yolks
- 1 teaspoon very finely chopped onion
- pinch of salt
- ¼ teaspoon mustard powder
- 1 tablespoon cider vinegar
- 2 generous tablespoons olive oil
- 2 tablespoons single cream
- herb-flavoured vinegar (tarragon or basil)
- mushroom ketchup or Worcestershire sauce (optional)

Pound the egg yolks and onion together in a mortar. When smooth, add the salt, mustard and cider vinegar. Mix well. Add the oil a little at a time, then mix in the cream. Stir in a few drops of herb-flavoured vinegar, and a little ketchup or Worcestershire sauce if desired. Taste and correct the seasoning.

A traditional five bar gate at Fulking Escarpment, West Sussex.

Hampshire strawberries were famous, partly because they were the first to reach the London market. The freshest, ripest strawberries are needed for this cake.

- 175g/6oz plain soft flour, plus extra for dusting
- 175g/6oz caster sugar
- pinch of salt
- 175g/6oz butter
- 1 egg
- 750g/1lb 10oz strawberries
- 100ml/3 ¹/₂ fl oz whipping cream

Mix the flour, sugar and salt. Rub in the butter, and stir in the beaten egg to make a soft, slightly sticky dough. Flour a work surface well, divide the dough in half and pat each one into a circle on a greased tray. Chill for an hour. Bake at 170°C/325°F/gas mark 3 for 30–35 minutes, until lightly browned; if the mixture spreads a lot, neaten it by trimming with a sharp knife whilst still hot. Cool on wire racks. About 2 hours before eating, place one cake on a plate and cover with strawberries – cut very large ones in half and put the other cake on top. Reserve a few fine berries for decoration.

Just before serving, whip the cream and cover the top of the cake. Decorate with the reserved strawberries and serve.

No-one really knows why these little cheese-cakes acquired this name. This is a late nineteenth-century recipe.

Makes about 24

- 500ml/18fl oz whole milk
- pinch of salt
- rennet
- 100g/3 ¹/₂ oz butter at room temperature
- 2 egg yolks
- 1 dessertspoon brandy
- 12 almonds, blanched and chopped
- 25g/1oz sugar
- 1 teaspoon ground cinnamon
- juice and zest of ¹/₂ a lemon
- 4 tablespoons of currants
- 250g/9oz puff pastry

The day before you want to bake the cakes, heat the milk to blood temperature, stir in a pinch of salt and add rennet as directed on the packet. When the curd has set and cooled, transfer it to a clean square of muslin or a jelly bag and allow the whey to drip out overnight.

Next day, rub the curd through a sieve with the butter. Beat in the egg yolks and brandy then stir in the almonds, sugar, a little cinnamon and the lemon juice and zest.

Roll the pastry out very thinly and cut into rounds with a plain cutter. Using a fork, prick the centres of the rounds lightly a few times, otherwise your maids may go head-over-heels in the oven. Line the patty tins with the rounds and put a generous teaspoon of mixture in each. Scatter a few currants on top of each one. Bake at 220°C/425°F/gas mark 7 for 7 minutes, until the pastry is risen and nicely browned. Best eaten warm from the oven.

A traditional dairy scene. The wooden pats would have been used to shape the butter with the scales used to measure out blocks.

KENTISH CORDIAL

A recipe from *The Country Housewife's Handbook.*

- 400g/14oz damsons
- 500ml/18fl oz water
- 175g/6oz elderberries, (about) 10 heads
- 1kg/2¼lb granulated sugar
- 2–3 cloves
- clear honey

Stone the damsons, retaining a dozen stones. Crack these to reveal the kernels, and add to the fruit. Pour 500ml/18fl oz boiling water over the stoned damsons and leave for 24 hours. Then bring to the boil and simmer for 15 minutes. Strain and pour the hot liquor over the elderberries. Leave for 24 hours then bring back to boiling again. Simmer for 10 minutes, strain and add the sugar. Add the cloves and stir in one teaspoon of clear honey per 500ml/18fl oz. Pour into sterilised bottles when cold.

LEMON REFRESHER CORDIAL

A recipe from the Young family at Grange Farm, Tichborne in Hampshire. A soft drink of the type which was often made for haytime, a season of hot, back-breaking work, now almost vanished, as many farmers opt for making silage.

- 900g/2lb granulated sugar
- 700ml/1¼pints water
- 2 lemons
- 20g/1oz citric acid (optional)

Put the sugar and water in a large pan. Add the grated rind and juice of the lemons and stir until the sugar has dissolved. Slowly bring to the boil, and the moment it reaches boiling point remove from the heat and allow to cool a little. Stir in the citric acid. Sieve the mixture and pour into sterilised bottles. Store in a cool place. Dilute to taste with cold water and serve with ice.

Citric acid helps preserve the cordial and heightens the acidity. It's easily available from a pharmacy. If the mixture is to be used quickly, the citric acid is not strictly necessary.

HAZELNUT TARTS

A few hectares of hazelnut 'plats' survive in Kent.

Makes about 30

- 100g/3½oz hazelnuts
- 60g/2oz mixed candied peel, finely chopped
- 2 egg whites
- 100g/3½oz caster sugar
- 3 tablespoons of water
- 400g/14oz puff pastry

Grind the hazelnuts, without removing their skins, in a food processor until they are mostly reduced to powder, but a few larger pieces are left. Mix with the candied peel and the egg whites, lightly beaten.

Put the sugar in a small pan and add the water. Bring to the boil, stirring all the time. Add this syrup to the hazelnut mixture and stir well.

Roll the pastry out thinly and cut into 30–36 rounds, re-rolling the scraps as necessary. Put them in patty tins with a spoonful of hazelnut mixture in each case. Bake at 200°C/400°F/gas mark 6 for 5 minutes, then lower the heat to 180°C/350°F/gas mark 4 for about another 10 minutes.

(left) 'Merry Weather' damsons ripening on a honey coloured wall.
(above) An array of traditional pastry- making utensils including tins, brushes and moulds.

PLUMS AND CREAM

Fruit was often simply stewed and served with custard or cream to make simple puddings. This is a slightly elaborated version, good made with the dark purple Early Rivers plums.

Serves 4–6

- 500g/1lb 2oz plums
- 200g/7oz sugar
- 150ml/5fl oz water
- 1 vanilla pod, split lengthways
- sour cream or crème fraîche to serve

Put the plums, sugar, water and the vanilla pod in a saucepan and cook very gently until the plums are soft. Remove the vanilla pod. At this point, you can either leave the plums whole or make a slightly more complex and elegant dish by coarsely sieving them or putting them through a *mouli-legumes*. If you do this, take a dozen plum stones, break them and add the kernels to the purée. Chill well and serve in glasses with a good spoonful of sour cream or crème fraîche in each.

CHERRY BUMPERS

A sort of cherry turnover, traditional to Buckinghamshire.

Makes 6

- 1 quantity shortcrust pastry butter and lard mixed, (see page 13)
- 1 tablespoon ground almonds
- caster sugar
- 1 drop bitter almond essence
- 250g/9oz fresh cherries, stoned

Roll the pastry fairly thinly and cut six 10–12cm/4–5in circles from it.

Mix the almonds with 2 tablespoons of caster sugar and work a drop of almond essence through the mixture with your fingers. Put a little of this almond mixture in the centre of each pastry circle, then divide the cherries between them. Brush round the edge of each piece with a little cold water and crimp the edges firmly to enclose the filling. Brush the top of each little parcel with water and then sprinkle with caster sugar.

Place on a greased baking tray and bake at 200°C/400°F/gas mark 6 for 12–15 minutes. Eat warm, but be careful when they are fresh from the oven as the cherries become very hot, or cold.

WESSEX

essex became synonymous with Dorset through Thomas Hardy's novels, depicting a deep-rooted rural community remote from the England of industrial cities. Even now, south Dorset – a maze of little valleys winding between spurs with the occasional church of grey stone or flint with a squat little tower – feels far removed from the twenty-first century. But Wessex is more than just Hardy country. It was the Saxon name for a kingdom which occupied roughly the land covered by Dorset, Somerset and parts of Wiltshire and Gloucestershire.

The area has a varied but attractive landscape, wrinkled up into ridges which run roughly north-west to south-east. On the west coast, the ground drops dramatically from Exmoor towards Porlock and Minehead, then undulates through the heavily wooded Quantock Hills down to the absolutely flat Somerset Levels. North of Bristol, the land flattens out into the vale of Berkeley where the Bristol

(previous page) Rolling fields on the Golden Cap estate, Dorset overlooking the sea.
(above) Farm buildings at Tivington Knowle, Somerset.

Channel funnels between flat low banks into the River Severn. To the north-east in the Cotswolds, the land begins to rise as limestone, once more. Towards the south, the land closes in to little valleys which wind towards the rivers Frome and Axe. The hills rise as one gets closer to the sea, with the Purbecks forming a narrow wave-like barrier, broken in the centre and guarded by the imposing ruins of Corfe Castle. This area has some of the most interesting and beautiful coastal scenery in Britain, as successive bands of clay and rock meet the sea and resist or erode, producing cliffs and landslips, little coves and stacks, and the long slender ribbon of Chesil Beach reaching out to the Isle of Portland. Much of this coast, and the farming hinterland, is owned by the National Trust.

The inhabitants of the coast are kept well aware of the sea by the mist and sudden squally winter gales, which bring a mingled, pleasing scent of sea air and heath. Inevitably, the west coast catches plenty of rain, but the climate is generally mild, and noticeably milder since the 1990s, according to Nikki Exton and Denise Bell, both tenants of the Golden Cap estate. This produces lush grass and dairy produce, especially in Somerset, where the Levels resemble green baize in summer. The area is also the traditional northern limit of the clotted cream tradition and cheesemaking becomes the primary dairy activity. It has been important in Somerset since the seventeenth century when Cheddar cheese was renowned for its excellence and size. The best farm-produced Somerset Cheddars have infinitely more character than blocks made by creameries, even those in the south-west. In the Gloucester area, milk from local Gloucester cattle, now a rare breed, helped the development of Gloucester cheese, double and single. Other cheeses are also produced in the area, including Caerphilly, which has been made in Somerset since the nineteenth century, Bath cheese, a soft square cheese, and the products of 'new wave' cheesemakers who have developed their own ideas, often using sheep or goat's milk.

The hillier land supports cattle and sheep for meat, and include local breeds such as North Devon cattle and Dorset sheep. Numerous other breeds are kept, including the rare Portland sheep, a 'primitive' or unimproved breed which is light and small. Pigs are also important (although the bacon industry at Calne, Wiltshire was founded in part on imported Irish pigs) but home-curing of bacon and ham is largely a thing of the past, partly because of regulations relating to killing and handling meat. Some butchers can still be relied on to stock Bath chaps, hog's puddings and chitterlings, and many local bakers make delicious, sticky lardy cakes.

The soft climate is good for orchard fruit. Apples are used for eating, cooking, and for cider-making. Interest in this drink has revived recently, and several makers produce versions made from single variety apple juices. Cider is sometimes used in cakes, and apple cakes rely on chopped apple for their moisture. Other baking traditional to the area includes the rich Bath specialities of Bath buns and Sally Lunn bread, both of which can be excellent.

Butcher shouldering large joint of organic beef from Hindon Farm, Somerset.

DENISE BELL'S SLOW-ROAST SHOULDER OF PORK

The essential ingredient for this is a very well brought up pig. At Heritage Prime in Dorset (www.heritageprime.co.uk), Denise rears her Tamworths for much longer than conventional farmers, giving very large, well-flavoured joints. To take advantage of this, you need to apply to her well in advance and be prepared to spend on quality. Otherwise, scout round your local farmers' market for someone who raises a traditional breed to a high welfare standard, and buy a piece with a decent fat cover.

Serves 16 or more

- 1 shoulder of pork (this will weigh about 9kg/20lb if you buy it from Denise)
- olive oil
- salt
- fresh thyme

Cooking time depends on size: a whole shoulder weighing 9kg/20lb takes 24 hours, a piece half that size 16 hours. However, the method works even on a relatively small piece if the cooking time is reduced proportionately. For example, give a shoulder weighing 2kg/4½lb 6–7 hours in the oven.

Take the pork out of the fridge an hour or two before cooking and allow it to come to room temperature. Pre-heat the oven to 250°C/475°F/gas mark 9. Make sure the skin of the pork is dry before rubbing it with olive oil, salt and fresh thyme; put a few sprigs of thyme underneath as well. Put the pork in the hot oven and leave it for 20–30 minutes. Turn the temperature down to 140°C/275°F/gas mark 1 and leaving it until almost the end of cooking time (a little longer won't matter). About 30 minutes before eating, turn the oven up to maximum again and give the meat a final blast for 15–20 minutes. The crackling is wonderful and the meat has a melting texture. Serve with a salad of bitter leaves and some good bread.

CHEDDAR PORK 'PIE'

Only a pie in the sense that shepherd's pie is - the covering is potato, not pastry.

Serves 4

- 2 tablespoons plain flour
- ½ teaspoon salt and some pepper
- 500g/1lb 2oz lean pork, diced in 1cm/½in cubes
- dripping or oil
- 150ml/5fl oz stock or water
- 2 tablespoons apple brandy (if this isn't available, whisky is the best substitute)
- 2–3 sweet apples, peeled, cored and sliced in rings
- 1 very large or 2 medium onions, peeled and sliced
- 4–5 large potatoes, peeled and sliced thickly
- 5–6 sage leaves, chopped

Mix the flour with the salt and some pepper and toss the pork in it. Smear the inside of an ovenproof casserole with a little dripping and put in the pork. Add the stock and apple brandy. Cover with a layer of apple rings, then onion, then potatoes; season these with a little salt and pepper and the sage. Then repeat, ending in a layer of potato. Grease a piece of foil with a little more dripping and cover tightly. Cook at 170°C/325°F/gas mark 3 for 2 hours. Uncover 30 minutes before the end of cooking, turn the heat up to 190°C/375°F/gas mark 5 to crisp and brown the potatoes.

(opposite top) Hardy's Cottage near Dorchester, Dorset. The novelist Thomas Hardy was born and raised in this cottage. His early novels *Under the Greenwood Tree* and *Far from the Madding Crowd* were written here.
(opposite bottom) Tamworth pigs at Heritage Prime, near Bridport in Dorset.

A fancy cockerel at Hindon Farm, Somerset.

SMOTHERED CHICKEN

A re-working of an old Dorset recipe for cooking rabbits.

Serves 4–6 depending on the weight of the chicken

- plain flour, for dusting
- 4 chicken joints, skinned, the legs divided into thighs and drumsticks, breasts cut in two
- 250ml/8 1/2 fl oz dry cider
- 200g/7oz fine white breadcrumbs
- 1 egg, beaten for binding
- 2 medium onions, chopped finely
- 1 teaspoon chopped, fresh thyme
- 1 teaspoon lemon zest
- salt and pepper
- 4–6 rashers lean bacon

Ovenproof dish to hold the chicken neatly in one layer

Flour the chicken and pack into the dish. Add cider until it half covers the chicken. Lay the bacon rashers over. Mix the breadcrumbs, onion, zest and thyme and season with a little salt and pepper. Add enough egg just to bind the mixture lightly (don't make it wet or try to press it together). Spoon over the meat. Bake gently 170–180°C/325–350°F/gas mark 3–4 for 1 1/2 hours, a little longer won't harm it. Towards the end of cooking, look to see if the cider is drying out, and if it is add a little more.

ESCALOPES OF PORK WITH APPLES AND CIDER

A recipe for local produce inspired by the French.

Serves 4

- 4 thin pork escalopes
- 3 tablespoons seasoned flour
- 30g/1 1/4 oz butter
- 2 tablespoons brandy
- 100ml/3 1/2 fl oz dry cider
- 2 apples, peeled, cored and thinly sliced
- 4 tablespoons double cream
- salt and pepper

Dip the escalopes in the seasoned flour. Melt the butter in a large frying pan. When it foams, add the pork and cook briskly, a couple of minutes per side. Remove to a warm plate. Pour in the brandy, scrape up any sediment on the bottom of the pan, then ignite it and burn off the alcohol. Add the cider and the apple slices. Allow to boil and reduce the cider to a quarter of the original volume (remove the apple slices before this point if they become tender). Add the cream to the pan and stir thoroughly, allowing it to boil. Taste for seasoning. Return the pork and any accumulated juices to the sauce, simmer for a minute or two and serve.

(above) Gloucester Old Spot pigs at Hindon Farm, Somerset.

HAM LOAF

One nineteenth-century wit defined eternity as two people and a ham. Here is one way to use the remains of a large piece when boredom has set in.

- 500g/1lb 2oz cooked ham, a quarter of which should be fat
- 125ml/4fl oz milk
- 60g/2oz crustless white bread
- black pepper
- ½ teaspoon ground mace
- ¼ teaspoon ground cloves
- 2 tablespoons fresh parsley, finely chopped
- 1 egg
- butter for greasing

A pâté terrine or loaf tin

Mince the ham or put it through a food processor until finely chopped. Bring the milk to the boil and soak the bread in it. Mix with the ham, grinding in some pepper and adding the mace, cloves and parsley. Taste and add a little salt if the mixture seems bland. Beat in the egg to bind.

Rub the inside of the pâté terrine or loaf tin with butter and pack the mixture into it. Cover with buttered paper or foil. Bake at, 180°C/350°F/gas mark 4 for an hour. Allow to cool, chill and turn out. Serve with salad.

LAMB OR MUTTON LIVER WITH ORANGES AND TOMATOES

'Oranges don't grow in England,' said Adam Simon at Tamarisk Farm, Dorset when we discussed the best way to cook the liver, which he sells along with the meat from his sheep flock. True. But then tomatoes, his preferred accompaniment, aren't native to the British countryside either.

Serves 4

- dripping or oil
- 1 large onion, chopped
- 1 tablespoon plain flour
- 1 teaspoon paprika
- ½ teaspoon ground cumin
- ½ teaspoon salt and pepper
- 400g/14oz mutton or lamb liver, cut into thin slices
- 4 tomatoes, skinned, de-seeded and diced
- 1 teaspoon orange zest plus the juice of a whole orange

Heat the dripping or oil in a frying pan and fry the onions fairly briskly for 10 minutes, stirring from time to time.

Mix the flour with the paprika, cumin, some salt and pepper and turn the liver slices in it. Move the onions to one side of the pan and add the liver, turning the slices to brown them on both sides. Then add the tomatoes, the orange zest and juice and a little water if the mixture seems on the dry side. Simmer gently until the liver is done to your taste – opinions vary as to whether it should be pink in the middle or well cooked.

Swaledale sheep from Hindon Farm, Somerset.

NIKKI EXTON'S DUCK EGG FRITTATA WITH SPINACH AND BUTTERNUT SQUASH

Nikki Exton keeps ducks and devised this recipe to show off their eggs and the vegetables from her farm. The colours are fantastic, and it tastes good too - duck eggs have a rich flavour. If you can't find duck eggs, use free-range organically produced hen eggs. It is important to cook duck eggs thoroughly.

- 1 small butternut squash, seeds, strings and peel removed, cut into 1cm/$\frac{1}{2}$in cubes
- 40g/1$\frac{1}{2}$oz butter
- 1 garlic clove, crushed
- 150g/5$\frac{1}{2}$oz spinach, picked over and washed
- 6 duck eggs, or 8 hen eggs
- freshly ground black pepper
- $\frac{1}{2}$teaspoon salt
- 50g/1$\frac{3}{4}$oz good-quality Cheddar cheese, coarsely grated
- 3–4 walnuts, chopped

A large frying pan with a lid

Put the prepared squash in an ovenproof dish with a little of the butter. Bake at 220°C/425°F/gas mark 7 for 20 minutes until just done.

Melt a little butter in the frying pan and add the garlic, then the spinach. Stir it around; the leaves will wilt dramatically. Remove from the heat when soft.

Beat the eggs, add plenty of pepper the salt and cheese. Stir in the cooked spinach, squash and garlic. Over a high heat, melt the remainder of the butter in the frying pan. When it begins to foam, pour in the mixture. Stir it a little to begin the cooking process. Then turn the heat down very low and leave to cook gently for 10–15 minutes, by which time the frittata should be mostly set but slightly runny on top. Put the lid on to complete the cooking: it is done when the top is set. Scatter with chopped walnuts. Serve hot or cold, cut in wedges.

BAKED EGGS WITH TARRAGON

This makes an excellent starter or tea-time dish.

Serves 4

- 4 eggs
- 125ml/4fl oz single cream
- salt and pepper
- 2 teaspoons fresh tarragon, chopped

4 individual ramekin dishes greased with a little butter

Mix the cream and tarragon, and season with salt and pepper. Divide between the ramekins. Break an egg into each dish. Bake at 180°C/350°F/gas mark 4 for 15–20 minutes until the whites are set but the yolks remain soft.

GREEN PEA SOUP

Pea soup is a traditional favourite, this recipe was recorded by Florence White in the 1930s but dates from the eighteenth century.

Serves 6

- 850ml/1 ½ pints water
- 300g/10 ½ oz green peas plus an extra 100g/3 ½ oz
- 2 sprigs fresh mint or fennel, leaves only, plus extra for garnishing
- 1 stem celery, chopped
- ½ Cos lettuce, shredded
- 1 teaspoon salt
- 1 teaspoon granulated sugar
- 40g/1 ½ oz butter
- ½ cucumber, peeled, cut into quarters, de-seeded and diced
- ½ large onion, finely sliced
- 1 tablespoon plain flour

Bring the water to the boil and add 300g/10 ½ oz of the peas, the mint, celery and the lettuce, plus the salt and sugar. Cook briskly for 20 minutes, then put the whole lot through a *mouli-legumes*. Return the mixture to the pan, add the other 100g/3 ½ oz of peas and bring back to the boil. In a separate pan, melt 25g/1oz of the butter and cook the cucumber and onion gently, without allowing them to brown. After 10 minutes, add to the soup.

Knead the remaining butter with the flour and drop it in small bits into the hot soup, stirring well. It should thicken a little but don't allow it to boil. Correct the seasoning. Serve with a little chopped mint scattered over the top.

(above) Fennel is an essential addition to a kitchen garden. All parts of the plant are edible

SPINACH AND SORREL SOUP

The market garden at Tamarisk Farm produces many unusual vegetables and herbs, including sharp-tasting sorrel, which is good in this soup.

Serves 4

- 40g/1 ½ oz butter
- 1 medium onion, peeled and finely chopped
- 200g/7oz young spinach leaves
- 150g/5 ½ oz sorrel leaves
- 20g/ ½ oz plain flour
- 350ml/14fl oz light chicken or vegetable stock
- salt and pepper
- 1 teaspoon grated horseradish (optional)
- 2 tablespoons double cream, whipped

Melt the butter in a saucepan and fry the onion gently until soft but not coloured. Add the spinach and sorrel leaves and allow them to wilt. Stir in the flour, then the stock, and bring to the boil. Liquidise or sieve and return to the pan. Taste and add salt and pepper as necessary and divide between bowls. Mix the horseradish with the cream and serve with a spoonful floating in each bowl.

WATERCRESS BUTTER

Special occasion teas - for birthdays, cricket, or visits by groups such as the W.I. - required mountains of pre-cut sandwiches. Most groups had their favourites. This watercress butter is also good with fish such as trout or cod.

- 60g/2oz butter
- 1 bunch watercress, leaves only, finely chopped
- pinch of salt and pepper
- squeeze of lemon juice

Cream the butter, add the cress and season to taste with salt, pepper and lemon juice.

Use as a spread for sandwiches, especially with ham or tongue, or serve with fish or eggs.

'Water Cresses, come buy my Water Cresses' from *Cries of London* by Thomas Rowlandson, 1799.

APPLE CAKE

Apple cakes frequently feature in books of Dorset and Somerset recipes. They are eaten warm, spread with butter or served with custard or cream. This version has been re-worked to emphasise the presence of the apples. Use a well-flavoured dessert apple.

Serves 8

- 150g/5 1/2 oz butter
- 150g/5 1/2 oz granulated sugar
- 2 eggs
- 300g/10 1/2 oz self-raising flour
- 1/2 teaspoon salt
- 1 teaspoon ground cinnamon
- 100ml/3 1/2 oz milk
- 400–450g/14oz–1lb apples, peeled and finely grated
- 1 tablespoon brandy or apple brandy
- 1 tablespoon caster sugar, ideally vanilla flavoured

A 20cm/8in cake tin, lined with non-stick baking parchment.

Cream the butter and sugar together until light and fluffy. Beat in the eggs. Sieve the flour, salt and cinnamon together and add this to the creamed mixture. Add a little milk to slacken off, but don't overdo it; the mixture should be on the stiff side.

Put half the cake mixture into the tin. Level it off, then make a hollow in the middle with the back of a spoon. Mix the grated apple with a spoonful of brandy or any other fruit-based alcohol and put these in the hollow. Don't let them touch the edges of the tin. Dollop the rest of the mixture over the top and smooth off, sealing the apple in the middle. Sprinkle the top with caster sugar.

Bake in a moderate oven at 190°C/375°F/gas mark 5 for 1 hour and 10 minutes. Serve warm with cream. The cake may be slightly puddingy in the middle, but should still taste good.

SALLY LUNN

There is no consensus on how this rich bread, associated with the town of Bath, got its curious name. What does matter is that it tastes good and shouldn't be ignored because commercial bakers have suddenly developed an obsession with *foccacia*.

- 1 teaspoon dried yeast
- 60ml/2 1/2 fl oz warm water
- pinch of sugar
- 125ml/4fl oz single cream
- 1 whole egg and 1 egg yolk
- grated peel of 1/4 lemon
- 250g/9oz strong plain flour
- 1/2 teaspoon salt
- butter for greasing

A deep cake tin 15cm/6in in diameter

Mix the yeast, water and sugar together and allow it to start working. When it froths, beat in the cream, egg and lemon peel. Put the flour in a mixing bowl and add the salt. Stir in the yeast mixture and mix everything well together. The mixture is too sticky to knead, but you should be able to form it into a flat round on a well-floured surface. Put the round of dough into the buttered tin. Set in a warm place to rise for 1–1 1/2 hours. Bake at 200°C/400°F/gas mark 6 for 15 minutes; if the bun seems a bit pale, turn the oven down to 170°C/325°F/gas mark 3 and give it an extra 5 minutes.

The proper way to eat Sally Lunns is to tear them in half, butter very liberally, put the halves back together and return the bread to the oven for a few minutes to melt the butter. Clotted cream can be used instead of butter.

PEAR TARTS

It's not traditional to use Sally Lunn dough as the base for tarts, but it tastes good.

Serves 8

- 1 quantity of Sally Lunn dough (see opposite), after rising
- 4 large ripe Conference pears, peeled, cored, quartered and thinly sliced
- 50g/1$^3/_4$oz butter
- brown sugar for sprinkling

Flour your hands and the work surface and divide the dough into 8 pieces. Make each into a thin disc 13–14cm/5–6in in diameter. Divide the pear between the dough circles. Dot with butter and sprinkle with a little sugar. Bake at 200°C/400°F/gas mark 6 for 10 minutes, then at 180°C/350°F/gas mark 4 for another 5 minutes, until the dough is crisp and golden. Serve warm, with cream if you must.

STRAWBERRY CIDER

A delicious summer drink.

- 500g/1lb 2oz strawberries
- 2 tablespoons caster sugar
- juice of 1 orange
- 500ml/18fl oz sweet cider, chilled
- ice

Crush the strawberries lightly. Place in a large bowl or jug. Scatter over the sugar and squeeze in the juice of the orange. Leave to macerate for an hour. Fill up with cider, add some ice and serve.

DISH OF CHEESE

Really an Edwardian recipe for a savoury - a rich, highly flavoured little something served right at the end of a meal. Use a really good quality Cheddar cheese.

Serves 4–6 as a light lunch dish

- 250g/9oz Cheddar cheese, sliced
- 50ml/2fl oz milk
- 150ml/5fl oz single cream
- 2 whole eggs and 1 egg yolk
- freshly ground black pepper

Put all the ingredients in a saucepan and heat gently, stirring continuously, until the mixture just comes to the boil. Serve in individual shallow dishes with rounds of toast and a salad of bitter leaves.

APPLE BUTTER

Made from any variety of apple, but particularly crab apples. I've given a recipe for a small amount. Use a preserving pan if making large amounts.

- 750g/1lb 10oz apples,
  a mixture of crab apples and Cox's work well
- 500g/1lb 2oz granulated sugar
- zest and juice of half a lemon

Wash the apples, quarter them and cut out any unsound bits, but don't peel. Put in a saucepan, add enough cold water to cover and simmer gently until soft and pulpy (this can take some time with crab apples). Sieve. Measure the pulp, the above quantity yielded about 850ml/1 $\frac{1}{2}$ pints. Return it to the pan and cook gently for an hour until quite thick; stirring from time to time.

Add the sugar, lemon zest and juice and boil rapidly until thick and no longer runny, which will take about 20 minutes. Stir constantly and make sure the mixture doesn't catch and burn, you may want to wrap you hand in a tea towel, as the mixture spits as it thickens. Pour into shallow containers and cover when cold.

A close view of 'Golden Hornet' crab apples.

The cliff edge of St Adhelm's Head, Isle of Purbeck, Dorset.

Green fields at Fontmell Down, Dorset.

RYE BREAD

Flour is sold by a few tenants in this area. One example is a wholewheat flour suitable for bread milled at Dunster Watermill near Minehead, Somerset. As well as this, archeo-botanists have got to work on extracting DNA from centuries-old wheat preserved in smoke-blackened thatch at Holnicote, Somerset. They have been experimenting with reconstituted wheat varieties with a genetic make-up similar to these late medieval types, which apparently make good bread. Rye and wheat were grown as a mixed crop known as maslin in the Middle Ages. In this recipe they make close-textured bread, good with butter and cheese.

- 1 dessertspoon dried yeast
- 50ml/2fl oz warm water
- 250ml/8 ½ fl oz milk
- 250g/9oz rye flour
- 250g/9oz wholemeal flour, plus a little for dusting
- 1 teaspoon salt
- 25g/1oz honey
- lard, butter or oil for greasing

A 900g-/2lb- bread tin

Add the yeast to the warm water and leave it to work. Warm the milk. Mix the flours and salt in a bowl and add the honey. When the yeast is frothy mix all ingredients together to make a dough and knead. Don't worry if it's slightly sticky, the ingredients can be mixed in a food processor, in which case they only need a minute to mix. Cover and leave to rise overnight – the dough will be fine left in a kitchen if it is cool, otherwise put it on the top shelf of the fridge.

Next morning, knock back the dough, flour a work surface and knead again. Shape into a loaf and put in the tin. Leave to prove for about an hour in a warm place.

Bake at 200°C/400°F/gas mark 6 for 15 minutes, then lower the heat to 190°C/375°F/gas mark 5 and bake for another 15 minutes. Turn the loaf out of the tin and return it to the oven, switched off, for a further 10 minutes, then allow to cool.

FENS AND EAST ANGLIA

East Anglia begins on the banks of the Thames estuary east of London, through the creeks and tidal marshes of Essex, smoothing into the long, straight coast north of Felixstowe, then curving back into the sands of the Wash. In this northern corner are the Fens, perfectly level black soil drained by a grid of water-filled ditches. If this resembles the Netherlands, it is partly because the topography is similar but also because Dutch helped to drain the Fens. A low ridge divides these from the flat land of east Norfolk and the wetlands of the Broads. South of Cambridge, the countryside rises a little and becomes less stern as it turns into Suffolk, a comfortable region of low rolling hills, pretty villages of half-timbered or pink-washed houses and huge churches.

The area is now thought of in terms of grain and vegetables, but this is not exclusively the case and never has been. Grain has always been important, and East Anglian farms were often large and wealthy. Wheat grows well here in the relatively warm, dry summers. East Anglia has the lowest average rainfall in the country, but some of the most bitter winter winds, sweeping in across the North Sea from central Europe. The coastline, under constant threat from erosion by the sea, includes salt-marshes, which support plants such as samphire, and sea lavender (which produces a distinctive pale yellow-green honey), shingle and sand, tidal inlets and the Broads. Wildfowling and fishing were traditional pursuits of the Broads and Fens, and landowners shot game, particularly partridges, which fed on grain crops. In Norfolk, some of the Breckland survives as a distinctive area of sandy heath; the rest has been forested or become arable farmland with hedge-like boundaries of twisted pines. The vast commercial rabbit warrens, which once provided income for this area, have gone in all except name. Further south, heathland also featured on the coast of Suffolk in an area known as the Sandlings which, together with the Essex marshes, were important for grazing livestock.

The obsession with monocultures of wheat or barley is a modern one; previously, the local economy had to be more self-sufficient. The traditional cattle breed of the area, Red Polls, were dual-purpose animals, bred for both beef and dairying. No-one would consider East Anglia dairy country now, but a delicious, soft cheese was made in the Ely area in the early twentieth century. Suffolk sheep, with their chocolate-coloured heads and legs are popular with farmers far beyond the county, and Suffolk also developed characteristic cures for hams and bacon, using black treacle and brown sugar. Rearing poultry, especially geese and turkeys, is a traditional East Anglian pursuit.

Vegetables and fruit also play their part in the rural landscape. They include cabbages, root vegetables and asparagus and apples, plums and soft fruit are important as there are two major jam-making companies in the area. A more unusual crop is mustard; although less is grown than formerly. Local baking traditions include little rusks known as Norfolk knobs, and dumplings, sometimes credited to Norfolk, sometimes to Suffolk, made from plain yeasted bread dough and cooked in boiling water.

(previous page) A winter view of Wicken Fen, Cambridgeshire. This is the last working wind-pump in the Cambridgeshire Fens.

(top) Thatcher's reeds cut and ready to use in Suffolk.
(bottom) North Brink beside the River Nene at Wisbech, Cambridgeshire.

ROAST PORK WITH GINGER AND MADEIRA

This is not a traditional recipe, although the use of Madeira is a nod back to the late nineteenth century, when it was popular.

Serves 6

- 1¹/₂ kg/3lb 5oz belly pork, the skin scored for roasting
- olive oil
- salt and pepper
- 20g/¹/₂ oz root ginger, peeled, cut into matchsticks
- 2–3 garlic cloves, bruised but not peeled
- 6 tablespoons Madeira
- 1 dessertspoon plain flour
- 150ml/5fl oz chicken stock

Leave the pork on a plate in the fridge overnight, uncovered; this encourages crisp crackling. Shortly before cooking remove it from the fridge, rub the skin with a little olive oil and sprinkle with salt. Put the ginger and garlic in a roasting tin and place the pork on top (try to ensure it covers them, otherwise they burn). Heat the oven to 220°C/425°F/gas mark 7 and put the meat in. Roast at this temperature for 30 minutes, then add most of the Madeira to the tin and turn the heat down to 150°C/300°F/gas mark 2. Leave it to cook gently for another 2– 2¹/₂ hours. Check occasionally to make sure it's not drying out (if it burns, it will taste bitter). Add the rest of the Madeira halfway through the cooking time.

When the meat is well cooked, lift it out of the tin to rest in a warm place. Drain the juices into a bowl and pick out the garlic cloves. Spoon off as much fat as possible, returning a tablespoon to the roasting tin. Add the flour and mix well over a low heat. Pour in the cooking juices and stir well, scraping in any sediment from the edges of the tin. Simmer until it thickens a little, and stir in the stock. Taste, correct the seasoning, and serve with some creamy mashed parsnip.

STEWED RED CABBAGE

A good accompaniment to sausages or a nice piece of roast pork.

- 1 small red cabbage
- 100g/3¹/₂ oz ham, in one piece
- 20g/¹/₂ oz butter
- 1–2 tablespoons muscovado sugar
- 75ml/3fl oz malt vinegar
- 200ml/7fl oz meat stock (broth from cooking bacon or ham is fine, as long as it's not too salty)
- pepper and allspice

Cut the cabbage in quarters, remove the stem and slice the remainder thinly. Put the ham and butter in the bottom of a casserole, and the cabbage on top. Add the sugar, vinegar and broth. Cook in a low oven 140°C/275°F/gas mark 1 for about 2¹/₂ hours. Watch it doesn't dry out. Taste and adjust the seasoning, adding salt if necessary and a little more sugar if desired. Grind a little pepper and allspice over just before serving.

Game pie, historically, would only be made on wealthy farms with large amounts of land over which the men could shoot. It can be made in the same way as pork pie (see page 134) with hot-water crust and jellied stock, using 450g/1lb meat from game and the same from pork. This version is a bit of a hybrid between a raised pie and a more standard short pastry version, devised when I had a lot of leftover game to deal with.

Serves 10 easily

For the sauce
- 50g/1 1/2 oz butter
- 2 level tablespoons flour
- 100ml/3 1/2 fl oz red wine
- 300ml/10fl oz stock, made from the bones and trimmings of game birds cooked with an onion and 1 bouquet garni
- nutmeg

For the pastry (see page 13 for the method)
- shortcrust pastry made from 450g/1lb plain flour
- 100g/3 1/2 oz butter
- 120g/4oz lard
- 1 teaspoon salt and 100ml/3 1/2 fl oz water

For the filling
- 450g/1lb venison, diced
- 450g/1lb assorted other game, cut off the bone (for example, pheasant, pigeon, partridge, rabbit, hare; cooked game can be used)
- 400–500g/14oz–1lb 2oz good pork sausage meat, divided into 10–12 balls
- salt and pepper
- egg, for sealing and glazing

A circular cake tin 20–22cm/8–9in in diameter, preferably with a loose bottom; line the base with greaseproof paper. Don't use a tin with an insulated base, or the pastry won't cook properly.

Make the sauce first. Melt the butter in a large frying pan. Brown the cubed venison, the sausage meat and the other game if it is raw. Remove, leaving as much fat as possible in the pan. Stir in the flour. Add the wine, scraping the bottom of the pan to pick up all the residues from the game. Pour in the stock and simmer gently for about 20 minutes. Taste, and add salt, pepper and a scrape of nutmeg. The sauce should be well seasoned. Turn into a basin and allow to cool to tepid.

Roll three-quarters of the pastry into a large circle and place in the tin, spread the pastry so it drapes over the sides. Ease it over the base, into the edges and up the sides, trying not to stretch it. You will have to make small pleats in places. Roll the remaining quarter ready to make the lid. Distribute the venison evenly over the base and top with the other game, arranging it so that each portion will get a share of something nice. Add the sausage meat balls. Pour in the sauce. Cover with the pastry lid, sealing with beaten egg. Trim, crimp the edges decoratively and add decorations of pastry flowers and leaves. Game pies should be very ornamental. Glaze with beaten egg.

Place on a heated baking tray in a hot oven, 220°C/425°F/gas mark 7 for 20–30 minutes (watch to see it doesn't brown too quickly), then turn the temperature down to 170°C/325°F/ gas mark 3 and cook for a further 1 1/2 hours. Remove the pie from the oven. Allow to cool in the tin overnight and serve cold.

HARE STEW

To do honour to a hare it should really be jugged, cooked in a large deep pot in a bain-marie for several hours, before using the animal's blood to thicken the sauce. A hare is a meaty animal, which will easily serve 6.

- 1 hare, cleaned and jointed
- 200g/7oz well-flavoured ham or bacon, chopped
  bouquet garni of parsley, thyme, marjoram
  and a bay leaf
- salt, pepper and ground mace
- 1 teaspoon of grated lemon zest
- 2–3 juniper berries, bruised
- 400ml/14fl oz well-flavoured stock, preferably beef
- 150ml/5fl oz red wine or port
- redcurrant jelly
- blood of the hare or 25g/1oz butter and 1 tablespoon
  plain flour, worked together into a paste

The hare should arrive complete with the pluck – kidneys, heart, lungs and liver. Examine the liver and make sure the gall bladder (a dark greenish sac) is removed. Otherwise, the pluck can be cooked with the hare, or the liver reserved, mashed, and added to the sauce at the end of cooking with the blood.

Scatter the ham or bacon over the base of a casserole. Place the hare on top of the bacon. Add the bouquet, a teaspoon of salt, some pepper and ground mace, the lemon zest, juniper berries and stock. Cover with foil, then the lid of the casserole. Cook at 170°C/325°F/gas mark 3 for 3 hours; then add the wine or port and cook for another 1 1/2 hours or so, until the meat is tender. Taste the juices adding more salt as necessary and a tablespoon or so of redcurrant jelly.

To thicken the sauce, if using the blood, mix with a little of the cooking liquid, then add it to the pot and stir gently over heat without boiling (the sauce will curdle if it boils). Otherwise, add the butter and flour mixture in little pieces and stir to incorporate them. Heat gently until the sauce thickens. Serve with baked potatoes or try the stew with a bowl of *parpadelle*, turned with a little butter and pepper.

POTATO CASE PIE

A recipe from Suffolk, recorded in the 1930s. Simple and good, this quantity serves 3-4 as a light meal.

- 500g/1lb 2oz floury potatoes,
  peeled and cut into chunks
- 25g/1oz butter, plus a little extra for greasing
- salt and pepper
- 50g/1 3/4 oz plain flour
- 120g/4oz ham, trimmed of any fat and minced
- 1/2 small onion, finely chopped
- nutmeg
- 3–4 sprigs of thyme
- Heaped teaspoon fresh parsley, chopped

An 18–20cm/7–8in round cake tin

Peel the potatoes, cut into chunks and boil until soft. Drain and mash with the butter; season with salt and pepper and work in the flour.

Mix the ham and onion and season with pepper, a scrap of nutmeg, the leaves picked from the thyme and the parsley. Stir well and add a couple of tablespoons water, or a little stock or gravy if you have it.

Generously butter the cake tin. Take two thirds of the potato mixture and spread it evenly over the base and about 2cm/1in up the sides. Put the seasoned ham in the middle. Use the remainder of the potato mixture to cover it, pressing the two layers together at the sides. Use the tines of a fork to make a nice pattern on top. Bake at 220°C/425°F/gas mark 7 for 30 minutes, by which time the edges and top will be deliciously brown.

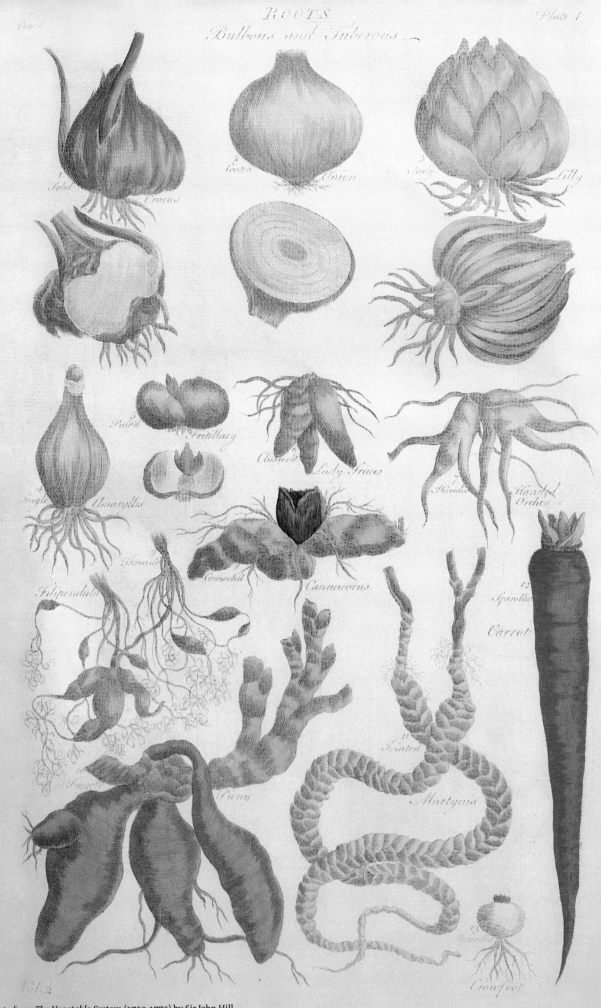

A plate from *The Vegetable System* (1759-1775) by Sir John Hill.

SPINACH SOUP

The original nineteenth-century recipe made a tasty but slightly muddy looking purée, to be served with suet dumplings. This makes a lighter, elegant green and white soup. Today's consumers might prefer croûtons to dumplings.

Serves 6–8

- 200g/7oz prepared weight of small white turnips, peeled and diced
- 200g/7oz onions, finely chopped
- 200g/7oz celery, finely chopped
- knob of butter
- 600ml/1 pint strong chicken stock
- 700ml/1 1/4 pints water
- 200g/7oz spinach, shredded
- 50ml/2fl oz single cream
- salt, pepper and nutmeg
- croûtons to serve

Sweat the turnip, onions and celery in the butter for 15 minutes. Add the chicken stock and simmer until soft. Put the mixture through a *mouli-legumes* or process to a purée. Return to the pan and add the water. Return to simmering and add the spinach, stirring slowly. Stir in the cream, add the nutmeg and season. Serve with a few croûtons in each bowl.

NORFOLK DUMPLINGS

The memoirs of Martha Blomfield, who grew up on a Norfolk farm in the late nineteenth century, inspired me to try the combination of hare stew and dumplings. The dumplings were eaten as a first course with the hare gravy, followed by the meat with numerous vegetables.

- 6 large dumplings
- 1 teaspoon dried yeast
- 150ml/5fl oz hand-hot water
- 250g/9oz plain flour, plus extra for dusting
- a scant teaspoon salt

Add the yeast to the water and allow it to froth. Mix with the flour and salt just as if making bread. When the dough is well kneaded, allow it to rise for about an hour.

Have a large pot of boiling salted water at the ready. Divide the dough into 6, make into balls and drop in the water. Keep them boiling for 20–25 minutes. The dumplings will expand a little as they cook. Drain and serve with the hare gravy; don't try to cut them, but pull apart with two forks.

PARSNIP FRITTERS

Root vegetables - carrots, parsnips, and beetroot - have long been a feature of the East Anglian landscape. This is an adaptation of a nineteenth-century method for cooking parsnips.

Serves 4 as a vegetable dish

- 400g/14oz parsnips, peeled and cut into chunks
- 25g/1oz plain flour
- salt and pepper
- 1 egg white
- oil or fat for deep frying

Boil the parsnips till soft, drain and mash. Stir in the flour. Season with a little salt and a generous grind of pepper. Beat the egg white to soft peak stage and stir into the mixture. Heat the oil or fat in a deep fryer and drop teaspoons of the parsnip mixture into it. Cook for 3–4 minutes until golden brown and slightly puffed. Drain on kitchen paper, sprinkle with salt and serve alongside grilled steak.

NORFOLK RUSKS

These little bread rolls are unusual in English bread-making, but are a well-established recipe in Norfolk.

Makes 18

- 100g/3¹/₂ oz butter
- 200g/7oz plain flour
- ¹/₂ teaspoon salt
- 1 teaspoon baking powder
- 1 egg
- 2 tablespoons milk

Rub the butter into the flour. Mix in the salt and baking powder. Add the egg and stir well, then add enough milk to make a fairly stiff paste. Divide into 18 pieces and roll each into a round a centimetre thick. Place on a greased baking sheet and bake at 220°C/425°F/gas mark 7 for 5–7 minutes until well risen. Remove from the oven and allow to cool for a short time, then score round the middle with a knife and pull each one in half. Return to a cool oven at 150°C/300°F/gas mark 2 until golden and dry all the way through (this takes about an hour). Cool and store in an airtight container. Eat with butter.

SUFFOLK CAKES

Delicious little cakes with a fine texture, similar to French madeleines. A mid-nineteenth-century recipe collected by Florence White.

Makes 24

- 100g/3¹/₂ oz butter
- 4 eggs
- 200g/7oz caster sugar
- finely grated rind of ¹/₂ lemon
- 100g/3¹/₂ oz self-raising flour, sifted.

Bun trays, well greased

Cut the butter into cubes, put in a mixing bowl and set in a warm place to soften. Keep working it until it is very soft and creamy.

Separate the eggs. Beat the whites to a stiff froth, then beat the yolks well. Stir the yolks into the whites and beat in the sugar and lemon rind. Gradually beat the egg mixture into the warmed butter (an electric hand beater is best for this). Be careful it doesn't curdle. Fold in the flour.

Half-fill each hollow in the bun trays and bake at 190°C/375°F/gas mark 5 for around 15 minutes, checking to make sure the cakes don't burn. Lift the cakes out of the bun tins and cool on a wire rack.

(right) Formerly used to drain the land, Horsey Windpump in Norfolk now offers striking views across the Broads.
(above) Dunwich Heath in Suffolk is an important conservation area for rare birds such as the nightjar.

Making and selling cheese was one way a farmer's wife generated income for herself. Few traditional British recipes for cheese are suitable for urban settings in which the ingredients have to be purchased, but this, used in the Fens to the east of Cambridge until the mid-twentieth-century, can be made quickly, in small quantities, and is delicious. Make it in summer, when the weather is settled and warm.

Crème fraîche gives a slight sourness when relying on pasteurised milk, and imitates a natural souring which develops in unpasteurised milk, or which is induced by cheesemakers with 'starters' of specially cultured bacteria.

You will need a deep metal or plastic tray, a solid wood or plastic board to fit inside it, a sushi mat and some moulds. Traditionally oblong wooden moulds were used. Now that the country craftsmen who used to make such objects have all disappeared, you have to improvise. An 850-ml/½- pint tinfoil pudding mould works quite well, even if the end result is not a traditional shape. Punch 8-10 evenly spaced holes, 5mm/½ in in diameter, round the sides of each mould.

The process takes around 3 days.

- 1½ litres/2½ pints whole milk
- 100ml/3½ oz whipping cream
- 100ml/3½ oz full-fat crème fraîche
- 1 teaspoon rennet

Start the cheese first thing in the morning. Wash the tray, board, sushi mat and moulds thoroughly with boiling water. Don't add detergent, as it can taint the cheese. Put the board on the tray, cover with the mat, and have the moulds ready.

Mix the milk, cream and crème fraîche in a bowl then pour into a large saucepan and heat to blood temperature, (think baby milk temperature).Pour the mixure back into the bowl, add the rennet and stir a few times. Then leave strictly alone for 30 minutes. Press the top gently with a clean finger: it should have set to a firm junket. Carefully spoon the cheese into the moulds, dividing it equally between them. Lots of whey will flow out of the moulds in the first few hours; carefully empty this off. Cover the moulds with a clean cloth and leave for 2–3 days, occasionally checking the amount of whey and emptying the tray if necessary. (If you have another tray, carefully move the board carrying the moulds into it.)

At the end of three days, unmould the little cheeses; they should have a slightly acid taste and a delicious rich texture. Since they are unsalted, they can be served either with fruit and sugar as a dessert, or with salad and biscuits as a light lunch or a starter.

BUTTERED WALNUTS

Most farmers' wives made simple sweets from time to time. This recipe is in honour of Wimpole Hall in Cambridgeshire, which holds trees belonging to the National Walnut Collection.

- 250g/9oz granulated sugar
- 45g/1 1/2 oz butter
- 100ml/3 1/2 fl oz water
- pinch of cream of tartar or 1 teaspoon lemon juice
- 100g/3 1/2 oz walnut halves
- 1 lime

Baking parchment or an oiled plate to put the sweets on

Put the sugar, butter and water in a heavy pan and melt together over a low heat. Stir until all the sugar crystals have dissolved, then boil without stirring to 154°C/309°F on a sugar thermometer. When a little of the mixture dropped in a bowl of cold water hardens instantly and breaks when you try to bend it, add the cream of tartar or the lemon juice. Remove the pan from the heat and dip the base in a bowl of cold water to prevent further cooking. Be careful, because the mixture is very hot.

Drop each walnut half into the hot sugar, flip over to coat and remove with a fork. Put on the paper or the oiled plate to cool. When cold, pack in an airtight container with sheets of baking parchment between the layers.

TREACLE CUSTARD TART

This is a sweet but addictive dessert.

- 1 quantity shortcrust pastry, use butter only (see page 13).
- 200g/7oz golden syrup
- 25g/1oz butter
- zest and juice of 1 lemon
- 2 eggs, beaten

An 18–19cm/7–8in round tart tin

Roll out the pastry and use it to line the tart tin. Cover the pastry with greaseproof paper, fill with beans and bake blind for 15 minutes at 180°C/350°F/gas mark 4. Remove the paper and beans and return to the oven for another 5 minutes.

Put the syrup and butter in a pan over a gentle heat. When the butter has melted, remove from the heat, and add the lemon juice and zest, then the eggs, mixing well. Pour into the pastry case and bake at 150°C/300°F/gas mark 2 for 30–35 minutes, until just set in the middle. Serve cool but not chilled.

The mysterious mounds of Sutton Hoo, an Anglo-Saxon burial ground, Woodbridge, Suffolk.

PEAK DISTRICT

The Peak District packs a lot of scenery into a small area, with two completely contrasting landscapes – the High or Dark Peak in the north and the White Peak to the south-east. The Dark Peak includes two high, brooding gritstone hills, Bleaklow and Kinder Scout, vast flat expanses of spongy peat bog, heather moorland and coarse grass with occasional weather-worn rock formations. The deep 'cloughs' or valleys contain square fields divided by charcoal-grey dry-stone walls and the occasional isolated farm. The White Peak has a completely different character – the underlying limestone gives vivid green pastures divided by pale stone walls. The streams here often vanish into underground caves, and some of the narrow little valleys are actually collapsed caverns. This area was mined for lead in the past, and in some places 'rakes' – ridges and spoil heaps created by mining – are evident. The spoil contains enough lead to be poisonous to grazing animals, and is sometimes tree-planted to prevent browsing. To the south-west lies an area of more mixed countryside. Hedged meadows and pastures fill the valleys running down to the flat land of Cheshire, Shropshire and Staffordshire. Higher up, moorland with gritstone walls and outcrops like the long spiky ridge of The Roaches occupies the north-east of Staffordshire. With the Potteries towns (see p.137) to the west, Manchester to the north-west, and Sheffield, Nottingham and Derby to the east, the Peak District is a popular destination for a day out.

This area marks the beginning of the Pennine hills, which stretch north to the Scottish border, and in common with much hill land, grazing of cattle and sheep is important. In the harsh environment of the Dark Peak, the higher ground is given over to managed heather moorland for grouse shooting. The South-Western Peak, with better pastures, produces sheep and cattle, and has some dairy farms. Dairying is much more important in the White Peak. Stilton cheese originated in Leicestershire in the eighteenth century and has been made at Hartington in Dovedale for at least a century. Another Midlands tradition which is also important in this area is the raised pork pie.

Sadly, the herb-rich fields with their beautiful spring flowers, characteristic of the limestone peak, have mostly vanished through late twentieth-century ideas about grassland management, but an interest in plants and their properties seems to be a feature of the area. The most vivid expression of this is the well-dressings; pictures and patterns made from leaves and petals impressed into clay, which several villages create every spring.

Like all farming communities, the Peak District favours home-baking. The climate in this area is too cool and wet to grow good wheat so oats are an important ingredient, as in many parts of upland Britain. Staffordshire and Derbyshire share a tradition of making large, yeast-leavened, oatcakes, generally bought from shops which specialise in them. Oatmeal also goes into thor or thar cake, a relative of Yorkshire parkin (see page 158). Pikelets, based on wheat flour, and made thick or thin, are also traditional. Bakewell Pudding, bought in the town or made at home, was for special occasions and 'wakes', the local name for a fair.

(previous page) Gritstone rock formations at Kinder Scout in Derbyshire.

(top) A hill stream, rushing between boulders on Kinder Scout, Derbyshire.
(bottom) Pastureland on Wolf's Hill, South Peak, Derbyshire.

STAFFORDSHIRE STEAKS

Braised steak recipes of this kind are out of fashion at present which is a shame as they taste good and can be left to look after themselves in a low oven.

Serves 2–3

- 500g/1lb 2oz rump steak
- beef dripping
- 1 large onion, sliced
- plain flour for the sauce
- 250ml/8^1/$_2$ fl oz boiling water
- 2 tablespoons mushroom ketchup
- salt and pepper

Cut the steak into 2–3 serving pieces. Fry in hot dripping until nicely brown on either side. Transfer to an ovenproof dish. Fry the onion in the same dripping and add to the steaks. Shake in a little flour to absorb the fat, then add enough water to make a sauce. Add the ketchup, taste and season with pepper and a little salt if necessary. Pour the sauce over the steaks and bake in a slow oven at 140°C/275°F/gas mark 1 for 2 hours. Serve with creamy mashed potato and crisply fried onions.

MUSHROOMS IN CREAM

The children's author Alison Uttley's Derbyshire childhood is beautifully evoked in her book *Recipes from an Old Farmhouse*, in which she describes cooking mushrooms in saucers of cream for breakfast or tea. Juicy, delicately flavoured field mushrooms are best. Cultivated mushrooms need a little help.

For 1 serving

- 6–8 button mushrooms
- salt and pepper
- 1 tablespoon fresh parsley, chopped
- 1–2 sprigs thyme, chopped
- 1 small clove garlic, crushed
- 75ml/3fl oz single cream

A small shallow ovenproof dish which will just hold the mushrooms

Wipe the mushrooms and trim the stems close to the caps. Place cap down in the dish. Sprinkle with salt and pepper and scatter the herbs and garlic over. Pour the cream over. Bake, uncovered, in a hot oven at 220°C/425°F/gas mark 7 for 20 minutes, or until the mushrooms are cooked. Baste the mushrooms with the cream halfway through cooking.

Serve on toast, or leave in the cooking dish and mop up the juices with fresh bread.

Longhorn cattle were commonly found all over Leicestershire, Staffordshire and Derbyshire in the eighteenth century. The National Trust cares for many rare breeds, including Longhorns, at Wimpole Home Farm, Cambridgeshire.

In the past pork pies showed local variations in recipe and method and a good pie was a source of pride to a housewife or local butcher. Skilled pie-makers raised the crust entirely by hand, giving it a slightly baggy appearance, or shaped the pastry over a cylindrical form which was removed to leave space for the filling. Using a cake tin gives more certain results, even if the pie loses a hand-made appearance.

Melton Mowbray in Leicestershire still produces a distinctive pie, and this recipe incorporates elements of that tradition - anchovy essence as a flavouring, and fresh meat instead of brined. The pastry recipe, from Derbyshire, is unusual in the combination of fats. Lard is the usual choice, and can be used for the total weight of fat in this recipe if desired. The method for the jellied stock was worked out by Jane Grigson as a better alternative to gelatine-fortified stock now used by many makers. The stock can be made in advance, but the pastry should be as fresh as possible.

Makes 1 large pie, which will serve 10

For the stock
- 2 pig's trotters
- bones, skin or trimmings from the pie meat
- 1 bay leaf
- 2–3 sprigs thyme
- 4 peppercorns
- 1 onion, stuck with cloves
- 3 litres/5 $\frac{1}{4}$ pints water

For the filling
- 1kg/2 $\frac{1}{4}$ lb pork, a quarter of which should be fatty, the rest lean; I use a mixture of shoulder and belly
- 1 teaspoon salt
- 1 teaspoon anchovy essence
- pepper
- 6–8 sage leaves, chopped

For the pastry
- 450g/1lb plain flour
- $\frac{1}{2}$ teaspoon salt
- 60g/2oz lard
- 60g/2oz butter
- 25g/1oz suet
- 1 egg, beaten

An 18–19cm/7–7 $\frac{1}{2}$ in round, sprung cake tin with a removable base

Place the stock ingredients in a large pan and bring to the boil. Skim well and simmer, covered, for about 3 hours. Strain the liquid into a clean pan and discard the debris. Boil the stock to reduce it to around 500ml/18fl oz. Leave to cool and jellify.

Cut a quarter of the leanest pork into cubes 1cm/ $\frac{1}{2}$ in across. Mince the rest coarsely – this is best done by hand with a sharp knife, as a mincer tends to compact the meat. Add the seasonings and turn well so they are evenly distributed.

Put the flour in a large bowl and add the salt. Measure the water into a pan and add the fats. Heat the pan, stirring, until the water has come to the boil and all the fat has melted. Remove the pan from the heat and stir the mixture into the flour. Use a wooden spoon at first, then, as it cools slightly, knead to make sure it is all incorporated properly. Cover the bowl and keep it in a warm place.

To raise the pie, take three-quarters of the pastry, still warm, and shape it into a disc. Put it in the cake tin and quickly raise it up the sides to the top, making it as even as possible and trying not to get the pastry too thick. The dough should be malleable – if it flops, it is too warm. Once the pastry is raised, pack the filling into it. Roll out the remaining quarter to make a lid and brush the edges with beaten egg. Trim any excess and crimp the edges. Make a small hole in the middle and cover it with a pastry rose. Cut leaves from the trimmings and use them to decorate the top of the pie. Brush with beaten egg.

Bake at 200°C/400°F/gas mark 6 for 30 minutes, then lower the heat to 170°C/325°F/gas mark 3 and bake for another 1 $\frac{1}{2}$ hours. Some gravy may bubble out of the pie, but don't worry too much about this – some recipes cite this as an indication that the pie is cooked.

At the end of cooking time, remove the pie from the oven and allow to stand for 20 minutes. Take the jellied stock, and if it has cooled off, re-heat to boiling. Ease off the pastry rose and pour in as much hot stock as the pie will hold. Replace the rose and allow the pie to cool. Wait 24 hours before cutting.

Looking into Chastleton Valley from Mam Tor, Derbyshire.

STILTON AND CELERY SOUP

Stilton cheese production is mostly centred on Leicestershire, to the south-east of the Peak District, but some is made in Derbyshire. Stilton and celery often appeared together on the Edwardian table; since the 1970s the combination has become a modern classic soup.

Serves 4–6

- 50g/1¾oz butter
- ½ onion, peeled and finely chopped
- 1 head celery, washed, trimmed of any leaves and chopped
- 25g/1oz plain flour
- 400ml/14fl oz chicken stock or vegetable stock for a vegetarian soup
- 400ml/14fl oz milk
- 250g/9oz blue Stilton, crumbled
- salt and pepper
- chopped parsley to serve

Melt the butter in a large pan. Add the onion and celery and sweat gently for 30 minutes but don't let them brown. Stir in the flour, then add the chicken stock and milk and simmer for another 30 minutes. Process to give a reasonably smooth texture (the celery will not break down entirely). Return to the pan and add the Stilton. Cook gently for a few minutes, stirring, until the cheese has melted. Taste and correct the seasoning. Add a little chopped parsley to each bowlful.

STAFFORDSHIRE OR DERBYSHIRE OATCAKES

A traditional food of the Peak District and the Potteries: pancake-like, thin and floppy. They were, and still are in the Potteries towns, made by specialists, but are also quite simple to make at home. The important point is to get the batter the right consistency.

Makes 7–8

- 1 teaspoon dried yeast
- 400ml/14fl oz hand-hot water
- 100g/3½oz fine oatmeal
- 40g/1½oz plain flour
- pinch of salt
- lard, vegetable oil or dripping for frying

Stir the yeast into the water, then add all the other ingredients and whisk to make a smooth batter as thick as double cream. Leave in a warm place for an hour.

Heat a heavy frying pan, or a griddle if you have one, on top of the stove. Grease it very lightly. Pour on enough batter to form a circle 16–17cm/6½in in diameter and let it cook gently. A few holes will appear in the top, which takes on a drier, set appearance. When the edges begin to lift a little, slide a spatula underneath the cake and flip it over. Allow to cook for a few minutes longer and then remove to a wire rack. Make all the pancakes this way. They can be stored in the fridge for 48 hours. To serve, re-heat either by frying in bacon fat and dishing up with a fried breakfast, or toasting both sides lightly under the grill and spreading with a little butter and some heather honey.

The fence marking the end of the National Trust's property in Mam Tor, Derbyshire.

PIKELETS

Similar in concept to the oatcakes (see previous page) and relatives of Welsh *crempog*. Much better than anything you can buy in the shops. Eat buttered for breakfast or tea.

Makes 24

- 200g/7oz plain flour
- 1 scant teaspoon salt
- 300ml/10fl oz milk
- ½ teaspoon dried yeast
- 2 eggs
- butter for greasing

Sieve the flour in a bowl, make a well in the centre and sprinkle the salt round the edge. Warm the milk to hand-hot in a pan and add the yeast. When it is frothy, pour into the flour and stir in, adding the eggs. Beat well to make a runny batter. Cover, and leave in a warm place for 1–2 hours.

Heat a griddle or heavy frying pan, grease it with a little butter, drop the batter in spoonfuls and cook until numerous holes appear in the top. Flip over with a spatula and cook briefly on the other side, until lightly browned. Toast under the grill before serving.

BAKEWELL PUDDING

This version was recorded by Alison Uttley. It's a lovely, rich dish for special occasions.

Serves 6

- thin puff pastry (a 250g/9oz block of ready-made pastry is ample)
- 100–150g/3½–5½oz raspberry jam
- 4 egg yolks
- 100g/3½oz melted butter
- 100g/3½oz caster sugar
- 100g/3½oz ground almonds
- 1 drop of bitter almond essence
- 2 egg whites

A deep oval dish of the type used for baking rice puddings – mine holds 850ml/1½ pints.

Roll the pastry out thinly and use it to line the dish, trimming the edges neatly. Spread a generous layer of jam over the base. Mix the egg yolks, butter, sugar, almonds and the almond essence. Beat the whites to a froth and stir in. Bake at 180°C/350°F/gas mark 4 for about 40 minutes. Serve tepid.

SUTTON WAKES PUDDING

This is like a hot version of summer pudding. A 'wake' was originally a vigil or watch observed to honour the local parish's patron saint. From an overnight vigil the 'wake' eventually became a celebration or fair, some of which could last as long as a week.

Serves 4–6

- 150g/5½oz self-raising flour
- 100g/3½oz fine white breadcrumbs
- 100g/3½oz salted butter, well chilled
- 750g/1lb 10oz mixed soft fruit – blackcurrants, strawberries, raspberries, redcurrants, gooseberries, rhubarb
- 80g/3oz caster sugar

A 1.2-litre/2-pint pudding basin greased with a little softened butter and sprinkled with a little Demerara sugar.

Mix the flour and breadcrumbs together. Using the coarse side of a grater, grate the cold butter into the mixture and distribute as evenly as possible. Add enough cold water tablespoon by tablespoon to make a firm dough. Roll the dough out and use it to line the prepared basin, reserving a quarter to make a lid. Add the fruit in layers, scattering sugar in between. Roll the remaining pastry into a circle, dampen the edges and place it over the filling, sealing well. Trim off any excess, cover with a double layer of foil and tie on firmly with string, making a loop over the top as a handle. Place in a large pan and add boiling water to come halfway up the sides of the basin. Steam for 2 hours. Serve hot with thick cold cream.

You can try unmoulding this pudding, but use a deep dish as lots of juice will flow out of it and be prepared for it to collapse.

'Carolina' Strawberry from *Lindley's British Fruits* 1846.

STAFFORDSHIRE FRUIT CAKE

One of the many variations of fruit cake found across the country.

- 450g/1lb currants
- 225g/8oz mixed candied peel, chopped
- 120g/4oz ground almonds
- 225g/8oz plain flour
- 160g/5½oz butter
- 160g/5½oz caster sugar
- 4 eggs
- 1 tablespoon black treacle
- 75ml/3fl oz brandy
- 1 teaspoon ground mace
- zest of 1 lemon
- 1 teaspoon baking powder
- 1–2 tablespoons milk

A 22-cm/8½-in cake tin, lined

Mix the currants, peel, ground almonds and 2 tablespoons of the flour together and set aside. Beat the butter and sugar together until light and pale. Beat in the eggs, one by one, alternating each with a tablespoon of flour. When all the flour has been added, warm the treacle and stir in with the brandy, mace, lemon zest and the baking powder. Add a little milk if the mixture seems very dry. Finally, stir in the fruit mixture.

Drop into the prepared cake tin, level the top and bake at 170°C/325°F/gas mark 3 for 2½ hours. This cake is better if allowed to mature for a couple of weeks before cutting.

BLACKBERRY JELLY

Blackberries grow everywhere in Britain, but the Peak District is a region which perhaps always had to rely more on wild foods than other parts of the country and the use of wild plants generally seems better remembered here.

- 750g/1lb 10oz blackberries
- 1 vanilla pod
- 1 sachet powdered gelatine
- 120g/4oz granulated sugar

Rinse the blackberries and put in a pan with the vanilla pod. Cover tightly and cook gently for a few minutes until they have yielded all their juice. Run through a jelly bag; retrieve and rinse the vanilla pod for use another day, discard the pulp and measure the juice. Make up to 500ml/18fl oz with water if the quantity is a little short.

Put the juice in a pan and heat gently until almost boiling. Put 100ml/3½fl oz juice in a cup or small bowl and add the gelatine, stirring to dissolve the powder. Add the sugar to the remaining juice and continue to stir until this, too, has dissolved. Remove the pan from the heat. Stir in the gelatine mixture. Pour into a suitable serving dish, or rinse a jelly mould in cold water and pour in the mixture. Allow to set and serve chilled.

(opposite) A hill stream at Edale Rocks, Derbyshire with a part of the Pennine Way in the background.

YORKSHIRE

Yorkshire divides very roughly into a hilly, wet western part and a lower, drier east. In the south-west, the hills are formed of millstone grit and the rocks of the coal measures. The land is not promising; steep, narrow valleys such as Calderdale rise to acid heather moorlands. Charcoal-coloured walls which once enclosed small green fields have now fallen into disrepair. Throughout this area, traces of the traditional pattern of farming can be seen in the grey gritstone farmsteads which pepper the landscape. The traditional methods of supplementing income from the land – wool processing and weaving, ironworking and coal extraction – gave rise to the industrial towns of the area. Market gardening became important, providing fruit and vegetables for the towns. Early forced rhubarb developed as a speciality to the Wakefield area, producing a fine and relatively high-value crop in the most unpromising conditions.

Further north, the broad glaciated valleys of the rivers Wharfe, Nidd, Ure, Swale and their tributaries provide excellent grazing for sheep and cattle. The underlying limestone makes for a sweet, herb-rich pasture with the classic Dales landscape of grey limestone walls and flat valley bottoms, threaded up with 'scars', (steep limestone outcrops with flat tops), stretching away across the hill tops, demarcating the grazing land of one parish from another. Cattle grazing these pastures produce excellent milk for cheesemaking, a tradition which dates back to the Middle Ages and probably originated with the monks of the great monastic houses at Fountains and Jervaux. Cheesemaking became especially important in Wensleydale, where farmers' wives made semi-hard cheeses in summer, to be kept for Christmas and the winter. Wensleydale cheese is still made, although most of it is produced in creameries. The land becomes bleaker and less populated as one progresses northwards through Swaledale, which gives its name to the local black-faced hill sheep.

To the east of the Pennines, in the flatter land of south Yorkshire and the vale of York, the rivers become contorted and sluggish, winding through areas of deep, rich soil to join the Humber estuary in that flat, no-man's land known to civil servants as Humberside. This territory, and the higher Wolds – the rolling chalk hills of eastern Yorkshire – is used for arable crops, especially sugar-beet and barley. The small but relatively high, heather-covered North York moors rise gently from the south and end in a precipitous ironstone scarp, binding the county to the north. The coastline provides dramatic contrasts; from the high creamy-white cliffs of Flamborough Head, south through the rounded boulder clay shoreline of Holderness to the slender comma of Spurn Point. The North York Moors and east Yorkshire catch the worst of cold north-easterly winds in winter, and may be snow-covered when the rest of the county is clear.

In the late eighteenth and early nineteenth century, the pasture lands of Yorkshire and Durham were renowned for producing cattle of prodigious size and the Craven Heifer, the Airedale Heifer and the Durham Ox are immortalised on numerous pub signs. Yorkshire still produces much good

(previous page) Moorland, farmland and woodland at Roseberry Topping, North Yorkshire.

beef although it is unlikely to come from Shorthhorn cattle, the breed favoured in the past. Beef dripping is used for frying in fish shops and can be bought in large white hunks from local butchers, many of whom also sell traditional potted beef. The native sheep breeds include Swaledales, the closely-related Dalesbreds, and the ringlet-coated Teeswaters and Wensleydales. Pigs were important in the weaving areas of south-west Yorkshire, where the Large White, now an important commercial breed, and the Middle White, rarer, but still favoured in parts of Yorkshire and Lancashire, developed in the nineteenth century. Ham-curing, using the dry salt cure which eventually became known as the York cure, was also important, and locally produced hams can be bought from a few butchers.

Baking included a tradition of using oatmeal, as the climate and topography of the north are not conducive to growing wheat. In the nineteenth century, the inhabitants of the West Riding ate havercakes, a distinctive form of oatcake, which requires considerable skill to make properly; sadly, the last maker in Yorkshire closed in 1999. Home-baking was of considerable importance. The oat tradition reappears in parkin, the local version of gingerbread. Wheat bread was also made at home, in large loaves or as flat 'oven bottom cakes', and lightly fruited teacakes. Cakes included 'spice cake' – large fruit loaves made for the tea table, and numerous other sponge cakes, buns and pies, including curd tarts. Pastry became more important in the East Riding, where rhubarb or apple pies were served for the farmhands' breakfasts in the early twentieth century.

(top) Yockenthwaite Top Farm surrounded by the rolling hills of the Yorkshire Dales National Park.
(bottom) A 'creep-hole' in a dry-stone wall in Swaledale, Yorkshire. The hole also known as a 'smoot', 'lunky' or 'hogg-hole' is designed to allow sheep to move between fields.

JULIA HORNER'S CUSHION OF LAMB

The Horner family have farmed at Redmire Farm, in the Upper Wharfedale estate, for over 80 years. Like other farmers on the estate they breed sheep, which provide foundation stock for commercial lamb production. The local sheep are horned, black-faced, raggedy-fleeced Dalesbreds and Swaledales, hardy enough to spend most of their lives grazing the herb-rich limestone pastures and heather moorlands of the nearby 'tops'. Some are pure-bred to continue the bloodlines for next year's stock. Others are cross-bred with Leicester or Suffolk rams, to provide mothers for another generation of lambs further down the dale. Inevitably, some are surplus to requirements. The 2001 foot and mouth epidemic forced Julia Horner to think creatively about marketing her lamb. A local butcher taught her methods for cutting and boning the meat, and a small abattoir a couple of miles away in Wensleydale agreed to work to her specifications. She uses the Dalesbred lamb, small-boned and sweet, for direct marketing and lets the cross-breds go to market. Her Dalesbreds provide the basis for some imaginatively cut joints including the 'cushion', a trimmed, boned shoulder neatly tied in a little square, and seasoned with bay and juniper.

A cushion of lamb will serve 4 nicely

- beef dripping or oil
- 1 cushion of lamb
- 200g/7oz each chopped onion, diced turnip, diced carrot and diced celery
- salt and pepper
- 100ml/3 1/2 fl oz stock or water

A casserole dish, preferably a small cast iron one in which the meat will fit neatly

Melt a little dripping or oil and brown the meat all over. Put the chopped vegetables in the bottom of the casserole and fit the meat on top. Add a little salt and pepper, and just enough water or stock to cover the bottom of the pot. Cover, and transfer to a very low oven 150–170°C/300–325°F/gas mark 2–3 for 3 hours.

Remove the meat to a warm dish and tip the rest of the contents into a sieve over a bowl. Strain, pressing the vegetables to extract the juices, then discard the vegetables left in the sieve. Skim off the fat and reduce the juices until syrupy by fast boiling. Check the seasoning.

Carve the meat in wedges as if cutting a melon, and serve with the sauce and freshly steamed vegetables. Serve some redcurrant jelly separately.

MRS INGLEBEY'S OATCAKES

An early twentieth-century recipe from Littondale, given to my mother by a local farmer's wife. Eat with butter or cheese.

Makes 36

- 300g/10 1/2 oz medium oatmeal
- 150g/5 1/2 oz plain flour
- 1/2 teaspoon salt
- 75g/2 3/4 oz lard or butter
- 4–5 tablespoons plain yoghurt (this should be buttermilk but yoghurt is a good substitute)

Put the dry ingredients in a bowl and rub in the lard or butter. Add the yoghurt or buttermilk and mix to a stiff dough. Press together and cut into three equal pieces. Roll each piece out until 5mm/1/2 in thick. Slide onto a baking tray (no need to grease) and cut each into 12. Bake at 180°C/350°F/gas mark 4 for about 15 minutes. Cool on a wire rack and store in an airtight container.

(left) Early morning mist creeps over Malharm Tarn, North Yorkshire.
(above) Sheep grazing amongst the stone walls and rocks of Darnbrook Farm, North Yorkshire.

A family favourite for Sundays and holidays. We always used a cut known locally as rands, and more widely as crop, bought on the bone.

Buy a handsome joint appropriate to the number of people expected, allow it to come to room temperature before cooking and season it with salt and pepper. Roast it in the conventional manner, starting in a hot oven 250°C/475°F/gas mark 9 for 20 minutes, and then lowering the temperature to 180°C/350°F/gas mark 4 for the rest of the time. Allow 20 minutes per 500g/1lb 2oz plus 20 minutes extra for medium-cooked meat (most cooks I knew tended towards well-done meat, but this is up to individual taste). At the end of the cooking time, remove the meat from the oven, put on a hot serving plate and leave to rest for 20–30 minutes whilst you concentrate on the gravy and Yorkshire pudding.

For the pudding
- 2 eggs
- 100g/3 $^1/_2$ oz plain flour
- pinch of salt
- 250ml/8 $^1/_2$ oz milk and water mixed half and half
- beef dripping from the roast

Traditionally, Yorkshire pudding is made in a large tin 24cm/9 $^1/_2$ in square – none of those silly little bun tin type efforts, although individual round puddings of 12cm/4 $^1/_2$ in in diameter are acceptable.

Mix the eggs, flour and salt, trying to avoid creating lumps. Then blend in the milk and water to give a mixture the consistency of thin cream. Try to do this a couple of hours ahead of time.

After the beef has been removed from the oven, turn up the heat to 220°C/425°F/gas mark 7. Add a tablespoon of dripping to the tin and heat it in the oven until smoking hot. Pour in all but 2 tablespoons of the batter (this should hiss spectacularly if the fat is the right temperature) and return the pudding to the oven.

To make the gravy, take the tin the beef was roasted in and spoon off any excess fat. Scrape up the sediment using any juices from roasting the meat and make up the amount of liquid to about 150ml/5fl oz with water or stock (in our household, it would have been water from cooking the vegetables). Let it bubble and then take it off the heat and stir in the remainder of the Yorkshire pudding batter. Keep stirring until the mixture thickens. Add a little more liquid as appropriate, taste, and adjust the seasoning.

A survival from the eighteenth-century
tradition of making meat or fish into pastes
to preserve under clarified butter. This often
appeared as a sandwich filling at festive teas.

Serves 2

- 250g/9oz stewing beef in one piece
- 1 bay leaf
- ½ teaspoon salt
- ½ teaspoon ground mace
- generous grind of black pepper
- 2 tablespoons sherry vinegar
- 60g/2oz butter, plus at least 60g/2oz for
  the top of the pot

Cut the beef into small pieces and add water up to the
level of the top of the meat. Stew gently with the bay leaf
for about 3 hours in a low oven 150°C/300°F/gas mark 2
until very tender. When well done, drain off the gravy and
reserve. Take out the bay leaf and shred the meat, removing
any very obvious bits of fat or gristle. Add the salt, half a
teaspoon mace, black pepper, vinegar and butter. Either
put the mixture through a mincer or process briefly, but
don't overdo it, adding some of the reserved gravy. The
mixture should be moist but not sloppy. Pack into ramekins
and clarify the remaining butter by heating in a small pan
until it foams. Allow it to stand so that the sediment can
settle at the bottom of the pan, then run the liquid butter
over the top of the meat to seal. Store in the fridge and use
within a few days.

As made by my grandmother for baking days,
when she needed a dish which would take care
of itself most of the time. She wouldn't have
added garlic, but it is an improvement.

Serves 4–6

- 750g/1lb 10oz stewing beef, trimmed of fat
  and gristle and cut in small slices
- 1 medium onion, chopped
- 1 tablespoon each of freshly chopped thyme,
  marjoram and parsley
- 2 garlic cloves, crushed
- salt and pepper
- 100ml/3½ fl oz water, stock or beef gravy
- 750g/1lb 10oz potatoes, peeled and thinly sliced
- butter
- 1 quantity shortcrust pastry made with lard
  (see page 13)

Put the meat in the bottom of a deep pie dish. Add the
onion, herbs, garlic and season well with pepper and half
a teaspoon of salt. Add the liquid and cover with a butter
paper or a piece of buttered tinfoil. Cook for 1 hour at
170°C/325°F/gas mark 3. Remove from the oven and layer
the sliced potatoes on top. Season with a little more salt,
dot with butter, cover with the paper or foil again and
return to the oven for another hour.

At the end of this time, the potatoes will be almost cooked.
Remove the dish from the oven and turn the heat up to
190°C/375°F/gas mark 5. Discard the paper. Roll out the
pastry and put it over the potatoes. Return the pie to the
oven for about 20 minutes, just long enough to cook the
pastry. Serve with steamed cabbage or broccoli.

ONIONS WITH CREAM SAUCE AND WENSLEYDALE CHEESE

An onion could provide a meal for a country-man or woman – a boiled or baked onion was a favourite with one of my aunts.

Serves 4

- 4 large, mild onions
- 25g/1oz butter
- 2 tablespoons plain flour
- 250ml/8½ fl oz milk
- 80ml/3fl oz double cream
- salt, pepper and a little nutmeg
- 60g/2oz Wensleydale cheese, grated

Peel the onions but leave them whole. Simmer gently in water until tender (this depends on size, but test after 30 minutes).

To make the sauce, melt the butter and add the flour to make a roux. Gradually blend in the milk and stir constantly until the sauce thickens. Allow it to cook gently on the lowest possible heat for 10–15 minutes. Add the cream, taste and add the seasonings. Split each onion in half and arrange in a shallow ovenproof dish. Pour over the sauce, scatter the cheese on top and flash under a hot grill to melt the cheese.

LAMB OR MUTTON ROGAN JOSH

Not, it could be argued, a traditional dish of farmhouse cookery, although curries have appeared in cookery books since the eighteenth century. When mutton fell out of favour in the 1960s, it didn't stop being produced, just found a new market - the Islamic butchers of our cities who buy it as a basis for curries.

serves 6

- 2 tablespoons vegetable oil
- 2 bay leaves
- 2cm/¾ in long piece of cinnamon stick
- 20 green cardamom pods
- 8 cloves
- 600g /1lb 4oz shallots, peeled and roughly chopped
- 6 cloves garlic, peeled and crushed
- 2cm/1in piece of fresh ginger root, peeled and finely grated
- 1 kg/2½ lbs shoulder of lamb or mutton, cut into cubes
- 1 generous teaspoon salt
- 2 teaspoons chilli powder
- 1 tablespoon paprika
- 500ml/1 pint natural full fat yoghurt
- 2 teaspoons good quality aromatic garam masala

A casserole or pan which can be used on top of the stove and in the oven

Heat the oil in the casserole; add the bay leaves, cinnamon, cardamom pods and cloves and cook gently in the oil for 1 minute. Add the shallots and stir well. Cook the mixture slowly for 25 minutes until the shallots are soft and slightly golden. Stir in the garlic and ginger and cook for a few minutes more. Add the meat, salt, chilli and paprika and continue to stir and cook for another five minutes or so. Then add the yoghurt and garam masala, mix well and bring to a simmer. If the stew seems on the dry side, add 100ml/3½ fl oz water and stir well. Cover and transfer to a moderate oven 180°C/350ºF/gas mark 4 and cook for about 2 hours. Stir occasionally and add a little more water or yoghurt if it seems to be drying. Just before serving, spoon off any excess fat and taste, adding more salt if necessary.

Winter in woodland on the North York moors.

CURD TART

On farms this was made using 'beestings' - the first milk a cow gives after calving, which curdles naturally when heated. This is unobtainable unless you happen to have a dairy herd. Alternative methods for making curd include heating milk with eggs or Epsom salts or using rennet, the method given here.

- 1 litre/1¾ pints whole milk
- rennet
- ½ quantity shortcrust pastry, use butter only (see page 13)
- 50g/1¾ oz butter
- 100g/3½ oz caster sugar
- zest of 1 lemon
- 1 egg
- 50g/1¾ oz currants
- 50g/1½ oz mixed candied peel
- 1 tablespoon rum
- nutmeg

A 20-cm/8-in pie dish or tart tin

The night before you want to make the tart, heat the milk to blood temperature and add the rennet. When the curd has set and cooled, put it into a square of clean muslin and drain overnight. It must be well drained. The next day, roll out the pastry and use it to line the tin.

Cream the butter, sugar and lemon zest together. Beat in the egg. Mash the curd with a fork, and stir into the mixture. Add the currants, peel and rum, and pour into the pastry case. Bake at 190°C/375°F/gas mark 5 for 40 minutes or until the filling is set. Grate a little nutmeg over whilst it is still warm.

ELLERBECK SPICE BREAD

A recipe collected in the 1930s by Mrs Arthur Webb. Ellerbeck is on the eastern edge of the Cleveland Hills.

Makes 1 loaf

- 1 dessertspoon dried yeast
- 200ml/7fl oz milk, hand-hot
- 325g/11oz strong plain flour
- ½ teaspoon salt
- 160g/5¾ oz Demerara sugar
- 1 teaspoon mixed sweet spice
- 120g/4oz butter
- 120g/4oz currants
- 60g/2oz sultanas
- 25g/1oz mixed candied peel
- 1 egg

A 900-g/2-lb loaf tin, greased and lined

Whisk the yeast into 100ml/3½ fl oz hand-hot milk with a pinch of sugar, and set aside until frothy. Mix the flour, salt, sugar and spice. Rub in the butter – not as thoroughly as for pastry, just until it is well distributed. Make a well in the middle and pour in the yeast mixture. Stir in a little of the flour from around the edge and leave it to work for a further 20 minutes. Then mix to a dough, adding more milk as necessary. Knead well, place in an oiled bowl, cover with a damp cloth and leave in a warm place for an hour or so. The mixture is unlikely to rise much.

Knock back and knead in the fruit, peel and egg. Shape into a loaf and place in the prepared loaf tin. Allow to prove for an hour; again, it won't rise very much. Bake at 180°C/350°F/gas mark 4 for 1 hour and 20 minutes; test with a skewer, and bake a little longer if necessary. Cool on a wire rack, slice and spread with butter.

TREACLE TART

This actually uses golden syrup, but was always known as treacle tart. A more elaborate version than the simple breadcrumb-and-syrup concoctions I knew as a child.

Serves 4–6

- ½ quantity shortcrust pastry, butter and lard mixed (see page 13)
- 50g/1¾oz currants
- 50g/1¾oz sultanas
- 50g/1¾oz mixed candied peel, chopped
- 60g/2oz brown breadcrumbs
- 1 apple, peeled and grated
- pinch of ground ginger
- pinch of mixed spice
- 2 generous tablespoons golden syrup, warmed
- juice and grated zest of 1 lemon

An 18-cm/7-in diameter pie tin

Roll out the pastry and line the tin. Add the currants, sultanas and peel. Mix together all other ingredients and spoon over the top, levelling neatly. Bake at 200°C/400°F/gas mark 6 for 20 minutes, then lower the temperature to 180°C/350°F/gas mark 4 for a further 10 minutes. Serve warm with cream or custard.

RHUBARB AND GINGER FOOL

This needs the early bright pink rhubarb, grown in special forcing sheds south of Wakefield.

Serves 4–6

- 600g/1lb 5oz forced rhubarb
- 100g/3½oz light brown sugar
- 250ml/8½fl oz whipping cream
- 4–5 pieces of preserved stem ginger, drained of syrup

Trim off the leaves and bases of the rhubarb stems, wash the stalks and cut into 2cm/¾in lengths. Place in an ovenproof dish, add the sugar, cover and bake for 30–40 minutes at 170°C/325°F/gas mark 3. Allow to cool.

Whip the cream until thick but not stiff and fold into the rhubarb mixture. Slice the ginger and stir in. Serve chilled.

Rhubarb growing in terracotta forcing pots. In the 1960's 93% of the world's forced rhubarb was grown in Yorkshire.

OATMEAL PARKIN

There are probably as many recipes for parkin as there are cooks who bake it. It comes in several varieties - cake-like, biscuit-like or made with oatmeal. This 1930s recipe from the Knaresborough area is unusual as it is based completely on oatmeal (most recipes require some flour) and includes rum.

Makes 24

- 500g/1lb 2oz medium oatmeal
- ¼ teaspoon salt
- ½ teaspoon bicarbonate of soda
- 2 teaspoons ground ginger
- 500g/1lb 2oz golden syrup
- 25g/1oz lard
- 25g/1oz butter
- 3 tablespoons rum
- 1 tablespoon single cream

Most recipes are worked out to fit an old-fashioned deep square Yorkshire pudding tin, 24cm/9½in square and 5cm/2in deep. Grease it well with lard or butter.

Mix the first four ingredients together in a large bowl. Warm the syrup with the lard and butter until the fats have melted, then stir in the rum and cream. Pour onto the oatmeal mixture and stir very well. Drop the parkin mix into the tin and bake at 150°C/300°F/gas mark 2 for around 1½ hours, until the mixture feels set in the middle and is just starting to pull away from the edges of the tin. Cool in the tin, cut into 24 pieces and lift out, sliding a spatula underneath. Parkin should be kept covered but not airtight for a couple of days before eating.

GINGER BISCUIT MIXTURE FOR PARKIN PIGS

Another recipe from Littondale (see page 147). Around 5 November, this type of mixture was used for making ginger pigs which were always known as parkin pigs.

Makes around 25 parkin pigs or 50 conventional biscuits

- 120g/4oz granulated sugar
- 60g/2oz butter
- 120g/4oz golden syrup
- 250g/9oz plain flour
- 1 teaspoon bicarbonate of soda
- ½ teaspoon baking powder
- 1 teaspoon ground ginger
- 1–2 tablespoons milk
- currants

Put the sugar, butter and syrup in a pan and set them over a low heat. Mix the flour, bicarbonate of soda, baking powder and ginger in a bowl. When the butter and syrup mixture is melted, add to the dry ingredients and stir well. Add a little milk, just enough to make a coherent dough. Dust a work surface with flour and roll out to a thickness of 5mm/¼in. Cut into pig shapes giving each one a currant eye. Bake on greased trays at 180°C/350°F/gas mark 4 for about 8 minutes (keep an eye on them, they scorch easily). Allow to cool a little before removing them with a spatula to a wire rack.

SPONGE CAKE WITH BILBERRIES

A very light, fragile sponge recipe from Husthwaite, recorded in a W.I. collection. It is important to beat the egg and syrup mixture for several minutes.

- 350g/12oz granulated sugar
- 100ml/3½ fl oz water
- 160g/5¾ oz plain flour sieved
- ¾ teaspoon baking powder
- 3 whole eggs and 1 yolk
- 100ml/3½ fl oz whipping cream
- 100g/3½ oz bilberries or other soft fruits such as raspberries or blueberries

A deep 22-cm/8½-in cake tin lined with greaseproof paper, the base sides buttered and dusted with caster sugar

Put the sugar and water in a pan and stir gently over a low heat until the sugar has completely dissolved. Then bring to the boil and switch off the heat. Sieve the flour and baking powder together.

Break the eggs into a large bowl and begin whisking them with a hand-held electric beater. After a few seconds start adding the hot sugar syrup, pouring it in a thin stream and whisking all the time. Continue whisking for 5 minutes, after which you should have a light, very foamy mixture. Sieve in the flour bit by bit, folding it in with a tablespoon. When the mixture is smooth, pour it into the prepared tin and bake at 180°C/350°F/gas mark 4 for 40 minutes. Test the top by pressing very lightly: it should feel firm to the touch and spring back a little, and the edges should be coming away very slightly from the sides of the tin. If in doubt, return to the oven for 5 minutes. Cool in the tin.

Carefully cut in half horizontally using a serrated knife and fill with whipped cream and soft fruit, preferably bilberries picked from the moors in July or August and sharpened with a squeeze of lemon juice.

RED TOMATO CHUTNEY

Noted in pencil in my grandmother's cookery book, she observes with a hint of pride that it 'is very nice and like sauce,' by which I think she meant tomato ketchup. Mine is not like that but still tasty.

- 1kg/2 1/4 lb tomatoes, skinned and cut in small chunks
- 150g/5 1/2 oz onions, chopped
- 300g/10 1/2 oz apples, peeled, cored and chopped
- 300g/10 1/2 oz granulated sugar
- 25g/1oz salt
- 1/2 a fresh red chilli, seeds and strings removed, chopped
- 1/2 teaspoon English mustard powder
- 1 dessertspoon coriander seed, ground
- 8 allspice berries, ground
- 350ml/12fl oz malt vinegar

Mix all the ingredients in a large pan. Simmer gently for about 2 hours until well reduced, thick and slightly brownish. Stir from time to time, more frequently towards the end of cooking, to make sure it doesn't stick. Pot in warm, sterilised jars.

MINT CHUTNEY

Mint sauce with a difference; the chilli and vinegar combination is good, especially after a few weeks mellowing, and would have appealed to my grandfather's generation.

- 50g/1 1/2 oz mint leaves, finely chopped
- 150ml/5fl oz cider vinegar
- 50g/1 1/2 oz granulated sugar
- 1 garlic clove, peeled and slivered
- 1 green chilli, cut in half

Put all the ingredients in a wide-mouthed jar, stirring well. Cork and leave on a sunny windowsill for 2 weeks, shaking occasionally. It keeps well in the fridge. Serve with roast lamb.

MINT PASTY

A Yorkshire variation on pastry and currants.

Makes 1 pasty

- 1 quantity shortcrust pastry made with butter and lard mixed (see page 13)
- 100g/3 3/4 oz currants
- 50g/1 3/4 oz raisins
- 50g/1 3/4 oz mixed candied peel, chopped
- allspice
- 2 bunches of fresh mint, finely chopped
- 2 tablespoons soft light brown sugar
- 15–25g/ 1/2 –1oz butter

Roll the pastry into a thin round a bit larger than a dinner plate and place it on a baking tray.

Cover half of it with the currants, raisins and peel. Sprinkle a little allspice over. Put the chopped mint leaves on top, scatter with brown sugar and dot with butter.

Wet the edges of the pastry, fold the other half over and pinch firmly to seal. Trim neatly. Bake at 200°C/400°F/gas mark 6 for 20 minutes. Best eaten soon after baking, whilst the scent of mint permeates the warm filling.

(right) Dawn over Yew Cogar Scar, North Yorkshire with Cowside Beck running through the valley.

My grandmother's recipe.

Makes 8

- 1 teaspoon dried yeast
- 500g/1lb 2oz plain flour
- 25g/1oz sugar
- pinch of salt
- 25g/1oz lard
- 25g/1oz currants
- 25g/1oz raisins

Mix the yeast with 100ml/3 $^1/_2$ fl oz tepid water and set aside until frothy. Put the flour, sugar and salt in a bowl and rub in the lard. Add the dried fruit. Pour in the yeast mixture and stir; add another 100ml/3 $^1/_2$ fl oz water and keep mixing to form a dough. Knead well, then cover and set aside to rise.

When doubled in size, knock back and divide into 8 pieces. Flatten each one into a disc 10–12cm/4in–4 $^1/_2$ in in diameter. Place on greased baking trays and allow to prove. When nicely risen bake at 220°C/425°F/gas mark 7 for 10–15 minutes. Eat warm with butter, or allow to cool, split and toast.

LEMON CURD

A preserve made in most farmhouse kitchens when eggs and butter were plentiful.

- 450g/1lb caster sugar
- 100g/3 $^1/_2$ oz unsalted butter
- zest and juice of 2 lemons
- 3 eggs, beaten and strained

In the top half of a double boiler mix the sugar, butter and lemon zest and juice. Cook over boiling water, stirring from time to time, until the butter has melted and the sugar crystals dissolved. Mix in the eggs and continue to cook, stirring constantly, until the mixture thickens (about 82°C/179°F on a jam thermometer). Pot in warm, sterilised jars and store in the fridge. Use within 6 weeks.

A 'north country' recipe, originally given by Florence White.

- 60g/2oz butter
- 500g/1lb 2oz self-raising flour
- 1 teaspoon salt
- 1 teaspoon cream of tartar
- $^1/_2$ teaspoon bicarbonate of soda
- 2 eggs
- 150ml/5fl oz double cream
- milk to mix – about 200ml/7fl oz

Rub the butter into the flour. Stir in the salt and the raising agents. Beat the eggs and cream together and stir in. Add enough milk to make a soft but not sticky dough. Knead lightly.

Roll out to approximately 2cm/1in thick and cut in rounds. Bake at 220°C/425°F/gas mark 7 for around 15 minutes.

Fantastic rock formations at Brimham Rocks, North Yorkshire, at a height of nearly 300m the rocks give spectacular views over the surrounding countryside.

The idea of the Scottish Borders is now confined mostly to the strip of land between Berwick-upon-Tweed and Gretna Green, but this hasn't always been so. Until the end of the Middle Ages, all the land between Yorkshire and the southern uplands of Scotland was fought over. This is apparent in some of the architecture of the region – the walls which surround Berwick, the houses of the village of Blanchland which all face inwards and the occasional pele tower – a fortified house. The absence of people is also, in part, a legacy of these centuries of low-level war, although other factors such as difficult topography play a part.

The Pennines continue northwards from Yorkshire through County Durham, becoming higher, bleaker and more lonely, though the flatter land towards the coast is well inhabited. West of Newcastle, the Tyne Valley cuts through the hills, followed along its length by Hadrian's Wall, a physical reminder that the Romans too had problems fixing a northern boundary to their Empire. To the north-east a narrow strip of flat land continues along the beautiful Northumbrian coast, past great medieval castles and the little island crag of Lindisfarne. an important monastery and centre of learning in the early Middle Ages. From the border at Berwick, the Cheviot Hills, after which the native sheep breed of the area is named, run south-west in a diagonal line, beginning as high bare grassy slopes, but forested around Kielder Water. The land drops to sea level again near the Solway Firth, and the Eden Valley opens to the south between the Lake District hills and the steep western slopes of the Pennines.

The flatter land on the east coast is an area of model farms with ranges of sturdy nineteenth-century buildings, one of which can be viewed at Beamish as part of the North of England Open-air Folk Museum, and rich arable land growing barley and other crops. Scattered across it are former mining communities whose traditions include an interest in competitive vegetable growing, especially giant leeks and onions. The wealthier inhabitants turned their glasshouses over to tropical fruit, as at Cragside. Inland, Teesdale and Weardale echo the Yorkshire Dales in their west-east orientation, but are more open, with fewer trees, fewer people and a harsher environment. Weardale, like Swaledale to the south, was once an important centre of lead mining. Some of the highest and roughest land is heather moorland, a habitat for grouse and other game. Given the height of the hills, (Cross Fell in the Pennines is almost 1,000m (3,200ft) and The Cheviot is not much lower), and the fact they lie so far north, the principal farming activity is bound to be pastoral, rearing lamb and beef. Along the coast, fishing and fish curing has always been important and remains so in places such as Craster and Lindisfarne.

(previous page) A winter view of Hadrian's Wall at Cuddy's Crag, Northumberland.

(top) The impressive remains of Dunstanburgh Castle, Northumberland. Built in the fourteenth century for the 2nd Earl of Lancaster, it was badly damaged during the fifteenth century Wars of the Roses – the struggle for power between the houses of York and Lancaster.
(bottom) Competitive vegetable growing was a great source of local pride in the North East.

HADRIAN'S WALL LAMB WITH ROOT VEGETABLES

Hadrian's Wall snakes across Northumberland, following a ridge of hard rock known as whin sill. Around the Roman fort of Housesteads, four farms occupy National Trust land, producing grass-fed beef and lamb, both new season and wether (grown on to 18 months old) as Hadrian's Wall Beef and Lamb.

This recipe can be used with a whole or half shoulder, or with neck of lamb, halved lengthways.

Serves 4

- 1 tablespoon oil
- $1/2$ teaspoon salt
- 700g/$1^1/2$ lb potatoes, peeled and cut into eighths
- 150g/$5^1/2$ oz turnips, peeled and cut into 1–2cm/$^1/2$–1in dice
- 150g/$5^1/2$ oz parsnips, peeled and cut in chunks
- 150g/$5^1/2$ oz carrots, peeled and cut in thick slices
- cloves from 1 head fresh garlic, peeled and left whole
- 1 small shoulder or two necks of lamb
- 4 sprigs of rosemary
- 8 sprigs of thyme
- redcurrant jelly to serve

Put the oil and salt in a roasting tin. Turn all the vegetables and the garlic in the oil until well coated. Put the meat on top, tucking the rosemary and thyme underneath. Sprinkle the surface of the meat with a little salt. Cover with tinfoil, sealing it round the sides of the tin. Cook at 230°C/450°F/gas mark 8 for 30 minutes, then turn the heat down to 140°C/275°F/gas mark 1 and leave it for $2^1/2$–3 hours.

Remove from the oven and turn the heat up to 220°C/425°F/gas mark 7. Put the meat on a warm plate and leave in a warm place. Discard the herbs. Pour as much of the fat and juice as possible from the roasting tin into a bowl, stir the vegetables around gently and then return them, in the tin, to the oven for 10 minutes to brown and crisp a little. Extract as much fat as possible from the juices. Chilling it briefly in the fridge solidifies the fat and makes it easier to remove but you need to re-heat it again.

Serve the meat, which will be falling off the bone, especially if you used lamb neck, vegetables and pan juices together, plus a little redcurrant jelly on the side.

JELLIED BEEF IN BROWN ALE

Brisket is not considered an elegant cut of beef, but it has an excellent flavour. Try it pot roasted - it makes the most delicious gravy. It works well in this dish, too.

Serves 8–10

- dripping or oil
- $1^1/2$–2kg/$3^1/2$–$4^1/2$ lb brisket, boned and rolled
- 300ml/10fl oz brown ale
- 1 pig's trotter
- $1^1/2$ teaspoons salt
- bouquet garni of bay leaf, parsley and thyme
- 1 garlic clove, bruised

A pot in which the meat fits neatly

Melt the dripping or oil and brown the meat all round. Add the brown ale and let it bubble. Put in the trotter, and add the salt, herbs and garlic. Finally, add cold water to about three-quarters of the way up the meat. Bring to the boil, cover with tinfoil and the lid of the pot. Simmer very gently for 3 hours, or cook in a low oven at 170°C/325°F/gas mark 3. It doesn't matter if it cooks a bit longer.

Allow the whole thing to cool, then lift the beef onto a separate plate, cover and cool completely. Bring the cooking liquor back to the boil and reduce by a third. Strain into a basin. Chill and lift off any fat which has risen to the surface. The stock underneath should have set to a firm brown jelly.

To serve, slice the beef neatly and arrange on a long dish. Chop the jelly and arrange down either side of the meat. Serve with salad and potatoes for a summer meal.

(left) A field of barley with the Flodden Field Monument in the distance, it was here that the English and Scottish armies fought a bloody battle in 1513. The Scottish king, James IV, was killed with as many as 5,000 of his men.
(right) Grass-fed sheep grazing near Hadrian's Wall, Northumberland.

HARE SOUP

There are several different recipes for hare soup in English and Scottish collections. This is a very aristocratic one, devised by a nineteenth-century French chef.

Serves 6

- 25g/1oz butter
- 100g/3 ½ oz lean bacon, cut into matchsticks
- 1 young hare, or the forequarters of a mature one, jointed
- 1 tablespoon plain flour
- 400ml/14fl oz red wine
- 500–600ml/18–20fl oz good beef stock
- 1 large onion, stuck with a few cloves
- 1 blade of mace and a few peppercorns
- bouquet garni of parsley, thyme, a bay leaf, marjoram, rosemary and basil
- ½ teaspoon salt
- 2 teaspoons redcurrant jelly
- 200g/7oz mushrooms
- fresh basil to serve

Melt the butter and add the bacon. Fry gently for a few minutes, then remove the bacon to your soup pan. Brown the hare joints in the same fat and add them to the bacon. Stir the flour into the remaining fat, add the wine and stock and scrape up any sediment. Add this to the bacon and hare along with the onion, mace, peppercorns, bouquet and the salt. Simmer gently for at least 1 ½ hours (an older hare will take up to 3 hours). Strain the soup into a clean pan. Pick over the debris, removing the meat from the hare bones. Cut into small pieces and add this to the soup, plus any bacon bits you find. Discard the remaining debris.

Stir in the redcurrant jelly and bring the soup back to the boil. Slice the mushrooms and add to the soup. Cook for a further 10 minutes. Serve with a little torn basil floating in each bowlful.

PEASE PUDDING AND HAM

Very much a north-eastern tradition, pease pudding can be bought in butcher's shops ready for heating up. This recipe is for those who have to start from scratch.

Serves 6

- 1 ham shank
- 450g/1lb yellow split peas
- 2 onions, finely chopped
- 25g/1oz butter
- 1 egg
- salt and pepper

Soak the ham and the peas separately overnight. The next day, drain and put everything in a pan and add enough water to cover. Simmer gently for 2 hours, by which time the peas should be a purée and the ham thoroughly cooked. Remove the ham and allow to cool.

To make the peas into a pudding, mix together the pea purée, butter and egg. Season well.

Pour into a greased pudding basin and steam for an hour. Turn out and serve with boiled ham or bacon.

A shooting party at Wallington, Northumberland in 1904.

BORDERS

LEEK PASTY

Leek puddings and pasties are a Northumbrian tradition. Try cheese in place of the bacon for a vegetarian version.

This makes a simple, light lunch or supper for 6

- 500g/1lb 2oz leeks, trimmed, washed and sliced
- 1 quantity shortcrust pastry, made with butter and lard mixed (see page 13)
- 200g/7oz lean bacon or ham, cut in small pieces
- 2 eggs
- 150ml/5fl oz milk or thin cream
- pepper
- egg or milk for glazing

A swiss roll tin

Plunge the leeks into boiling water for a minute, then drain them in a sieve. Press a plate over the top to remove as much liquid as possible, and leave to drain whilst you prepare the pie.

Roll two-thirds of the pastry thinly and use to line a swiss roll tin. Scatter the ham or bacon over the base. Put the drained leeks on top. Beat the eggs with the milk or cream and some pepper and pour over. Roll the rest of the pastry thinly, cover the pie and seal, crimping the edges with a fork. Brush over with beaten egg or milk. Bake at 200°C/400°F/gas mark 6 for 20 minutes.

LITTLE CHEESE TARTLETS

A variation on the theme of cheese baked with breadcrumbs, quite common in British cookery.

Makes 24 tartlets

- 1 quantity shortcrust pastry made with butter and lard mixed (see page 13)
- 200g/7oz good Cheshire cheese
- 25g/1oz butter, plus extra for greasing
- 2 eggs
- 50g/1 3/4 oz fine white breadcrumbs
- 150ml/5fl oz double cream
- pepper and a pinch of salt
- pinch of cayenne pepper

Grease the mince pie tray or patty tins well. Roll the pastry out thinly and divide between the pastry cases. Next grate the cheese finely, melt the butter and beat the eggs well. Mix all the ingredients together, and divide between the pastry cases. Bake at, 220°C/425°F/gas mark 7 for 10–15 minutes. Serve warm.

SINGIN' HINNIE

A cake from the Northumbrian tradition of griddle baking; plain but very more-ish.

Makes two large cakes 20cm/8in in diameter

- 400g/14oz plain flour
- generous pinch of salt
- 1 teaspoon baking powder
- 100g/3 1/2 oz lard
- 100g/3 1/2 oz butter
- 140g/4 1/2 oz currants
- 2–3 tablespoons milk to mix
- butter, brown sugar and nutmeg for serving

Mix the flour, salt and baking powder. Rub in the fat, stir in the currants and mix to a dough using the milk. Divide in two and roll out to about 1cm/ 1/2 in thick rounds. Heat a griddle or a large heavy frying pan, grease lightly with lard and put a round on to cook. Keep an eye on the heat, which needs to be fairly moderate. It may take up to 15 minutes to bake. When the underside is brown, turn and cook the other side. Split crosswise, butter well, sprinkle with brown sugar and nutmeg and eat warm.

(above right) The kitchen at Cherryburn, Northumberland. The artist and naturalist Thomas Bewick (1753-1828) was born here, he is buried at Ovingham churchyard, just across the river from Cherryburn.

BROWN SCONES

Excellent served with sour cream and smoked fish - try them with Craster kippers.

Makes 18 small scones

- 200g/7oz wholemeal flour
- 200g/7oz plain flour
- 1 teaspoon bicarbonate of soda
- 1 teaspoon cream of tartar
- generous pinch of salt
- 100g/3 $^1/_2$ oz lard or butter
- 1 egg
- 4–6 tablespoons milk

Sieve the dry ingredients together. Rub in the lard or butter. Beat the egg and stir in, and add enough milk to make a coherent dough. Divide the dough into two equal pieces and form each into a neat square, rolling out until about 1cm/ $^1/_2$ in thick. Trim the edges so they are reasonably neat and place each piece on a greased baking tray and cut into nine pieces. Bake at 220°C/425°F/gas mark 7 for 10 minutes. Eat warm.

ANNE HORNE'S BUTTER TART

Also known as Borders tart, there are numerous variations of this north-eastern favourite. This one actually came to me via Whitby, where Anne's family lives.

- 1 quantity shortcrust pastry (see page 13)
- 75g/2 $^1/_2$ oz melted butter
- 300g/10 $^1/_2$ oz currants or mixed fruit
- 300g/10 $^1/_2$ oz Demerara sugar
- 3 eggs
- 2–3 drops vanilla essence

A 22-cm/9-in flan dish

Use the pastry to line the flan dish. Mix all the other ingredients together and pour into the case. Bake at 200°C/400°F/gas mark 6 for 30–40 minutes. Serve warm with whipped cream.

MRS WATSON'S ICED GINGER SHORTCAKE

Mrs Watson's family farm is at Longwitton, where the hills start to rise towards the Cheviots. These shortcake fingers are delicious.

Makes 16 fingers of shortcake

For the shortcake
- 200g/7oz butter
- 100g/3 $^1/_2$ oz caster sugar
- 250g/9oz flour (Mrs Watson recommends half plain, half self-raising)
- 1 $^1/_2$ teaspoons ground ginger

For the icing
- 75g/2 $^1/_2$ oz butter
- 1 tablespoon golden syrup
- 1 teaspoon ground ginger
- 60g/2oz icing sugar

A shallow 22-cm/8 $^1/_2$ in square tin

Cream the butter with the caster sugar. Mix the flour with the ginger and work into the creamed mixture. Press into the tin and bake at 150–170°C/300–325°F/gas mark 2–3 for 40 minutes, until golden brown.

Whilst the shortcake is still warm, make the icing. Melt the butter and syrup together. Add the ginger and icing sugar and stir thoroughly to give a smooth mixture with no white patches of icing sugar. Pour over the cake. Cut into fingers whilst still warm, then leave to cool in the tin.

LAKE DISTRICT

On a map of Cumbria the Lakes radiate from a
central point like spokes of a wheel, with the
highest mountains clustered in the middle. East-
west routes are difficult, through a few constricted passes,
and north-south ones, threaded between lake shores and
steep slopes, are not much easier. Even so, tourists have
been visiting since the eighteenth century, attracted by
the drama of the scenery. Yet the remoteness of the area,
combined, with some local pride, managed to keep local
distinctiveness alive when it was vanishing elsewhere.
The National Trust has been a landowner here for over
a century, and is responsible for about a quarter of the
land area and the farmsteads on it. Its properties include
Townend, a long, low, stone and slate house in the local
style, once belonging to a Cumbrian 'statesman' (farmers
who owned their own land), which gives an idea of the
traditional way of life in this area. The farming community
remains close-knit and was badly affected by the foot and
mouth epidemic of 2001.

Inevitably, given the height of the hills and their
situation on the west coast, the climate is wet, and, in
winter, often snowy; but it is easy to forget this on a
summer's day when the trees are in full leaf, the hills
dappled with cloud shadows and the little fields on the
flat valley floors full of summer grass. Each lake has its
own character: Windermere and Coniston Water are
long and narrow, and open to the south; Wastwater is
set in a steep, scree-bound valley; Buttermere is almost
unbelievably pretty, and Ullswater has a feeling of gentle
melancholy. Given the lakes and the streams which feed
them, one might expect freshwater fish. Sadly, char, once
considered a speciality of Windermere, has been over-
fished and few are now taken. On the coast to the south
though, there are brown shrimps which are delicious when
simply boiled or potted under spiced butter.

Sheep, especially the native Herdwick which are mostly
confined to this area, graze the tops of the highest hills.
Cattle for beef, and to a lesser extent milk, are also important.
On the flatter land which fringes the western edge of the
hills, a tradition of pig-keeping and ham-curing flourishes.

This is not country for growing wheat and like much of
highland Britain oats were once important, although the
'clapbread', thin dry oatcakes which took their name from
being 'clapped out' by hand on a flat board have vanished.
Baking traditions include numerous variations on tea
breads and other dried fruit-based goodies. Little bread rolls
flavoured with caraway, known by the old name of 'wigs'
were made in Hawkshead and Kendal. A distinctive and
very good gingerbread is made in Grasmere. The Cumbrian
tradition of brown sugar, rum and spices, very apparent in
sweet foods, derived from the West India trade once vital
to the little ports on the west coast.

Vegetables, beyond plots for domestic use, don't feature,
nor is fruit of importance, with the exception of the
damson. These little plums were planted in the hedgerows
of the valleys draining the southern lakes, and used for
jams and pickles and by one brewery for flavouring beer.

(previous page) Autumn mist over Derwentwater and Skiddaw, Cumbria.

(top) The River Cocker in full flow through the Buttermere Valley, Cumbria.
(bottom) Castlerigg Stone Circle has been tentatively dated from 3200BC. Although impressive, the 38-stone site has left few archaeological clues to its meaning and significance to ancient man.

As well as producing tasty lamb and mutton, the Herdwick's fleece is being used for producing hard-wearing carpets.

SLOW-ROAST HERDWICK MUTTON AND *SALSA VERDE*

Herdwick sheep have been grazing the Lake District fells for centuries and are now a rare breed, mostly confined to this area. They have a distinctive appearance, with pale heads, small curved horns and rusty brown or grey fleeces. The importance of sheep is reflected both in the lamb- or mutton- based 'tatie pot' (see page 183) and in special dishes made for busy days like at sheep-clipping time. Grazing sheep also help to maintain the bare, grassy slopes of many of the hills. Their survival owes much to Beatrix Potter, a sheep farmer as well as a children's writer, who left her land to the National Trust on condition that Herdwicks were grazed on it in perpetuity. Their meat is used in several traditional Lake District recipes, but local butchers and farmers such as Hazel Relph at Yew Tree Farm and the Flock-in Café in Borrowdale (www.borrowdaleherdwick.co.uk) have developed their own ideas for cooking it, including 'herdi-burgers'. The ingredients of *salsa verde* echo the English traditions of caper sauce with mutton and mint sauce with lamb. I first came across the idea of serving it with Herdwick mutton at a Heritage Feast cooked by Joy Davies and Gareth Jones for Slow Food.

If you're lucky enough to acquire a leg of Herdwick mutton, cook it very slowly at 140°C/275°F/gas mark 1, allowing 1 hour per 500g/1lb 2oz. Otherwise support your region's farming community and source some good-quality lamb from your local area. *Salsa verde*, which includes both capers and mint, recalls the English traditions of caper sauce with mutton and mint sauce with lamb.

- a generous handful each of mint, parsley, basil
- 1 small garlic clove, crushed
- 2 tablespoons capers, rinsed
- 2 tablespoons Dijon mustard
- 2 tablespoons red wine vinegar
- 8 tablespoons olive oil
- salt

Wash the herbs and pick the leaves off, discarding the stalks. Blend all ingredients together, taste and season. Serve with Herdwick mutton or lamb, roasted or grilled.

MUTTON AND BARLEY BROTH

A way of using one of the less elegant cuts of lamb or mutton. The garlic and lemon are not traditional, but give the soup a lift.

Serves 4–6

- 1 ½ kg/3lb 5oz scrag end, chopped into slices
- 2 litres/3 ½ pints cold water
- 120g/4oz carrot, scraped and sliced
- 60g/2oz turnip, chopped
- 1 medium onion, peeled and chopped
- 4 sticks celery, chopped
- 60g/2oz pearl barley
- salt and pepper
- chopped parsley, a small garlic clove and a scrape of lemon zest for serving

Put the meat in a pan and add the water. Gently bring to the boil and skim off all the impurities. Add the vegetables. Simmer gently for 2 hours, adding a little more water if it seems to be evaporating. At the end of the time strain the broth into a bowl and allow to cool. Pick the best of the meat off the bones, then discard these and the vegetables. Skim all the fat off the top of the broth. Put it in a clean pan with the pearl barley and simmer gently for about 40 minutes or until soft. Add the meat and season with salt and pepper.

Crush the garlic, mix with the parsley and a little grated lemon zest – just enough to tell it's there – divide the broth and barley between bowls and add the parsley mixture just before serving.

(above) Beatrix Potter with Tom Storey, her sheperd at Hill Top Farm, Cumbria with one of their prize Herdwicks.

PICKLED RED CABBAGE

This is always served with tatie pot.

- 1 medium red cabbage, outer leaves removed
- salt
- 600ml/1 pint malt vinegar
- 1 tablespoon granulated sugar
- 1 tablespoon pickling spice

Quarter the cabbage and remove the stem. Shred it, sprinkle with salt and leave to stand overnight. The next day, rinse the salt off and drain thoroughly. Boil the vinegar, sugar and spice together for 10 minutes, then allow to cool a little. Pack the cabbage in warmed, wide-mouthed jars and strain the vinegar mixture over. Tie down and leave for a week before using.

GILLIAN TEMPLE'S HERDWICK TATIE POT

Tatie pot is a standby for every farmer's wife in Cumbria, a good-tempered stew of meat, black pudding and potatoes. Every one has their own variation, and the potatoes may be sliced, cut in chunks or halved for the final layer. Gillian Temple remarks that she makes this dish for hungry farmers returning from gathering sheep on the fells. It's the kind of food which is a necessity when farming in Eskdale, to the west of Hardknott Pass.

Serves 6–8

- 1kg/2$^1/_4$lb neck or shoulder of Herdwick lamb, cut into large pieces
- 200g/7oz stewing beef, cut into small pieces
- 4 carrots, peeled and chopped
- $^1/_2$ a swede, peeled and chopped
- 1 large onion, peeled and chopped
- flour, salt and black pepper
- 200g/7oz black pudding, sliced
- 6 large potatoes, sliced
- 500ml/18fl oz strong beef stock

Place a layer of meat on the bottom of a casserole. Cover with a layer of carrot, swede and onion, and sprinkle with flour, salt and pepper. Then add the rest of the meat, plus the black pudding in a layer. Cover with the remaining swede, carrot and onion, and sprinkle with flour and seasoning. Top the casserole with the sliced potatoes and salt and pepper these. Pour the stock over to just below the level of the potato layer. Cover and cook at 190°C/375°F/gas mark 5 for at least 3 hours. Remove the lid for the last 30–40 minutes to crisp the potato.

The dish can be kept hot in a low oven for much longer, and will not spoil.

(above) Holstein Friesian cows at Lower Sizergh Farm, Cumbria.

CARLISLE STEAK

An updated version of a dish which Mrs Arthur Webb noted as 'guaranteed to keep out the chilliest cold' when she came across it in the 1930s. She served it with fried potatoes, but I prefer a mixture of mashed potato and parsnip. Well-matured rump steak is best for both flavour and texture. The meat needs 6-12 hours marinating.

Serves 4

- 4 tablespoons malt vinegar
- 4 tablespoons soy sauce
- 1 tablespoon muscovado sugar
- 100ml/3½ fl oz bitter beer
- ½ teaspoon ground allspice
- 4 pieces of rump steak
- 1 tablespoon plain flour, plus extra for dusting
- oil for frying
- 25g/1oz butter
- chopped parsley to finish

Mix the vinegar, soy, sugar, beer and allspice in a wide shallow bowl and put the steaks in it. Cover and leave on one side; turn the meat from time to time. When the time comes to cook the meat, lift it out and allow the liquid to drain off it for a few minutes. Reserve the marinade.

Blot the surface of the steaks dry with kitchen paper and dust with flour. Heat a smear of oil in a heavy frying pan, and when hot put the steaks in. Allow to sizzle for a few minutes, turn, and continue until they are done to your taste. Remove from the pan and let them rest on a warm plate whilst you make the sauce. Take the pan the steaks were cooked in and add the butter to the cooking residues. When it has melted, stir in a tablespoon of flour. Add the marinade, stirring well to incorporate the roux and any bits stuck to the pan. Add a little stock or water if it seems too thick. Pour over the steaks and garnish with chopped parsley.

SAUCER PIES

As one travels further north, pie fillings depend less on pork products and more on beef, or mutton, like these little pies. The mutton or lamb can be cooked or raw, but give the latter a longer initial cooking time.

Makes 4 little pies using saucers as moulds

- beef dripping
- 2 shallots, chopped
- 1 garlic clove, crushed
- 300–350g/10½ oz–12oz cooked neck of lamb or mutton, trimmed of fat and chopped fairly fine
- 120–150g/4-5½ oz mushrooms, sliced
- 3–4 tablespoons of stock made from the bones of the lamb
- 2–3 tablespoons fresh parsley, chopped
- 2–3 sprigs fresh thyme, chopped
- salt and pepper
- 1 quantity shortcrust pastry made with lard (see page 13)
- a little gravy from lamb or beef (not essential, but a good addition)
- milk or beaten egg to glaze

Melt the dripping and fry the shallots and garlic gently for a few minutes. Add the meat and cook over a moderate heat. Stir in the stock. Season with the herbs and a little seasoning. Stew gently giving pre-cooked meat 10 minutes, raw meat about 40 minutes. If you have some good gravy left over from a roast, add this at the end and allow it to bubble for a few minutes. Taste and correct the seasoning. Leave to cool.

Divide the pastry into 8 and roll each piece into a circle as big as a saucer. Press 4 pieces into saucers and divide the filling between them. Top with the reserved pastry circles, seal, trim and crimp the edges with the tines of a fork. Brush over with glaze. Bake at 220°C/425°F/gas mark 7 for 20–25 minutes.

Shaggy Redhaired Longhorn cattle graze with sheep below the Kirkstone Pass, Ullswater Valley in Cumbria.

CUMBERLAND GRIDDLE CAKE

Plainer and thinner than Northumbrian singin' hinnies (see page 173), but very good.

- 75g/2 ¾ oz plain flour
- pinch of salt
- generous pinch of baking powder
- 25g/1oz butter, plus a little extra for greasing
- 60–75ml/2 ½ –3fl oz milk or thin cream

A griddle or a heavy frying pan

Mix the flour, salt and baking powder. Rub in the butter. Mix to a dough with the milk or cream. Flour a work surface lightly and roll out to a circle about 5mm/¼ in thick.

Heat the griddle and grease lightly with a little butter. Put the cake on it and cook gently for 10–15 minutes. When golden brown underneath, turn and cook for another 5–10 minutes on the other side or until golden. Cut into squares, split and serve buttered on a hot dish.

CUMBERLAND SAUSAGE IN BEER

Cumberland sausages should be full of coarse-cut meat and a bit of seasoning, and come in one long coil, not as links. They are excellent grilled or fried, but cooking them in beer produces a good gravy.

Serves 4

- 25g/1oz beef dripping or 2 tablespoons oil
- 500–600g/1lb 2oz–1lb 5oz Cumberland sausage in a long piece
- 1 onion, peeled and sliced
- 1 tablespoon plain flour
- 300ml/10fl oz beer, preferably not too bitter
- salt and pepper

Try to use a frying pan or casserole in which the sausage will fit in a neat coil. Melt the dripping or oil and cook the sausage briefly on both sides, just enough to brown it. Remove it to a plate and add the onions to the fat and cook gently until soft but not brown. Sprinkle in the flour and stir well. Stir in the beer. Let it bubble and reduce a little. Add the sausage and cook very gently for 30–40 minutes. Taste the gravy and season if necessary, but the sausage will probably have provided enough salt. Serve with mashed potatoes.

Peggy Ellwood's recipe for a plain but very good fruit loaf of a type well known in the Lake District, in which the dried fruit is soaked in tea before the loaf is mixed.

- 300ml/10fl oz strong tea
- 450g/1lb mixed dried fruit (sultanas, raisins and currants)
- 175g/6oz soft light brown sugar
- 350g/12oz self-raising flour
- 2 large eggs, beaten
- 3 tablespoons milk
- 2–3 drops vanilla essence and a little mixed spice (optional)

A 900-g/2-lb loaf tin, well greased and lined

The night before you want to make the loaf pour the tea over the dried fruit and leave to soak.

Next day, add all the other ingredients and mix well. Pour into the loaf tin and bake on the middle shelf of the oven at 170°C/325°F/gas mark 3 for 1 1/2 –2 hours. Leave to cool in the tin. Slice and serve well buttered.

CUMBERLAND CLIPPING TIME PUDDING

Christine Edmund, who sent this recipe, says that this was one of the special dishes provided on sheep clipping day when all the neighbours came to help. The quantities given will serve about 8 people (unless they've been clipping sheep, in which case it might not stretch as far).

- 150g/5 1/2 oz pudding rice
- 1.5 litres/2 1/4 pints milk
- pinch of salt
- 80g/3oz sugar
- 1/2 teaspoon cinnamon
- 60g/2oz butter
- 100g/3 1/2 oz currants
- 100g/3 1/2 oz raisins or sultanas
- 1 egg, beaten

Pour some boiling water over the rice to blanch it, then drain. Put in a large pan with the milk, salt, sugar and cinnamon and simmer very gently, stirring occasionally, until the rice is tender (about 40 minutes). Then transfer to an ovenproof dish and stir in the butter, dried fruit and beaten egg. Bake on 190°C/375°F/gas mark 5 for 20 minutes.

WIGS

A 'wig' was the name given to a small bread roll from the late Middle Ages and well into the nineteenth century. They were usually a little richer than plain bread, and both Kendal and Hawkshead were noted for them, although they now seem to be forgotten. A shame, because they are good. This recipe was recorded by Florence White.

Makes 16

- 100ml/3 1/2 fl oz warm water
- 2 teaspoons dried yeast
- 500g/1lb 2oz strong plain flour
- 1/2 teaspoon salt
- 50g/1 3/4 oz lard
- 50g/1 3/4 oz soft light brown sugar
- 1 tablespoon caraway seeds
- 150ml/5fl oz milk

Add a pinch of sugar to the warm water and set the yeast to work until frothy. Put the flour and salt in a bowl and rub in the lard. Stir in the sugar and caraway seeds. Add the yeast mixture, the milk, and a little more water if necessary to make a dough. Knead well, then leave to rise in a warm place.

When doubled in size, knock back and divide into 16 pieces. Roll each into a small, flat round and place on a greased baking tray. Allow to prove, then bake at 180°C/350°F/gas mark 4 for 15–20 minutes.

Herdwick ewes and lambs being gathered together for marking at Birk Howe Farm, Little Langdale, Cumbria.

DAMSON PICKLE

A more common use for damsons is to pickle them, for eating with cheese or cold mutton. Here is one among many recipes.

- 700g/1¹/₂lb damsons, washed and dried
- 600ml/1 pint vinegar (malt or distilled malt)
- 350g/12oz granulated sugar
- 2–3 cloves,
- 1 small stick of cinnamon
- 1 blade of mace

Prick the damsons all over with a darning needle and put them in a bowl. Boil the vinegar, sugar and spices together and pour over the fruit. Cover and leave overnight. Next day, drain and reserve the liquid and re-boil. Pour over the fruit again and leave for a second night. Repeat this the next day. On the final day, boil the fruit and the liquid gently for 5 minutes. Try not to let the skins break. Pot in warm sterilised jars, cover and keep for at least a month before eating, preferably longer.

DAMSON SAUCE

This damson sauce recipe came from Marion Hayton in Penrith. To say someone is 'saucy' in Cumbrian dialect means that they are cheeky.

- 250g/9oz damsons, washed and dried
- 250ml/8¹/₂fl oz port
- 2 cloves
- generous pinch of ground cinnamon
- 25g/1oz soft brown sugar
- 3 level tablespoons redcurrant jelly
- juice of 1 lemon and 1 orange

Put the damsons, port, cloves, cinnamon and sugar in a pan and bring to the boil. Cover and simmer for 15 minutes then add the jelly and fruit juice. Mix thoroughly and bring back to the boil. Cool and sieve. Excellent served over meringues and whipped cream.

A still autumn afternoon at Buttermere. The scenery in Buttermere is notable for being both dramatic yet surprisingly tranquil.

MARY EDMUND'S DATE SANDWICH

Simple, quick and satisfying baking of this sort fills cake tins all over the country. Recipes came from all over - from family or friends, the W.I., newspapers or the back of packets, or out of people's heads - and were quickly absorbed into family traditions.

Makes 16 fingers

- 250g/9oz dried stoned dates
- 250ml/8 1/2 fl oz water
- 140g/5oz rolled oats
- 140g/5oz self-raising flour
- 140g/5oz granulated sugar
- pinch of salt
- 140g/5oz butter, plus a little extra for greasing

A swiss roll tin

Break up the dates and simmer with the water for about 20-25 minutes, or until soft.

Mix the oats, flour, sugar and salt in a bowl and rub in the butter. Grease the tin and press in half the oat mixture. Spread the softened dates over the top, then scatter over the rest of the oats. Level neatly. Bake at 180°C/350°F/gas mark 4 for 30–35 minutes. Cut into fingers whilst warm, but leave in the tin until cool.

GINGERBREAD CRUMBLE

Grasmere gingerbread can also be good in a pudding.

Serves 6

- 500g/1lb 2oz fresh raspberries
- 140g/5oz butter
- 250g/9oz self-raising flour
- 120g/4oz soft light brown sugar
- 1 teaspoon ground ginger
- 1/2 teaspoon lemon zest

Put the raspberries in a baking dish. Rub the butter into the flour, then stir in the remaining ingredients. Cover the fruit with this mixture (don't press it down). Bake at 180°C/350°F/gas mark 4 for 30 minutes. Serve tepid with cold cream.

GRASMERE GINGERBREAD

Grasmere gingerbread is sold from a little shop in the village. It is very delicious, and the recipe is secret. This version comes from Marion Hayton.

Makes 16 fingers

- 225g/8oz butter
- 450g/1lb plain flour
- 225g/8oz light brown sugar
- 1 teaspoon bicarbonate of soda
- 1 teaspoon cream of tartar
- 2 teaspoons ground ginger
- pinch of salt
- 1 tablespoon golden syrup
- butter for greasing
- granulated sugar to finish

Rub the butter into the flour. Add the other dry ingredients and mix well. Add the syrup and rub into the mixture until it is crumbly. Grease a baking sheet and press the mixture on to it in a block 1cm/1/2 in thick. Don't be alarmed if it's crumbly. Bake at 150°C/300°F/gas mark 2 until golden brown. Sprinkle with a little granulated sugar. Allow to cool for 15 minutes, then cut into fingers.

View from Grange Crags in Borrowdale. Brandlehow Woods, was the National Trust's first acquisition in the Lake District in 1902. Today the Trust protects 11,800 hectares of the surrounding countryside.

WALES

Wales is, of course, a separate country with language, customs and, to some extent, food all of its own. From north to south, the country divides into three basic areas of superb mountain landscapes: Snowdonia, a mass of shattered volcanic rock cut across by u-shaped, glaciated valleys; the Cambrian mountains, running down the centre, which vary in their ruggedness but are still spectacular, and in the south the high but smooth slopes of the Brecon Beacons – sandwiched, confusingly, between Black Mountain to the west and the Black Mountains to the east. Other smaller mountain areas such as Cadair Idris provide equally spectacular scenery. Much of the Welsh coast is undeveloped, varying from flat tidal estuaries such as Llanrhidian Sands, which separate the Gower Peninsula from the mainland, to the rock-strewn beaches of Marloes Sands near Milford Haven.

The north, apart from the Dee estuary and the slate quarries of the Conwy coast, is almost exclusively rural, the landscape moving through the relatively gentle hedged pastures of the Vale of Clwyd to the dramatic lake and mountain scenery of Snowdonia, with tawny and black peaks and ridges fit only for grouse, deer and the hardiest of sheep. South-east from Snowdonia, the Llyn Peninsula points into the Irish sea, with little bumpy hills above flat, almost treeless fields and a rocky shore. Anglesey, too, is relatively flat, with small fields divided by hedges and boulder walls.

In south-east Wales the landscape is a post-industrial one, where the spoil heaps of the Rhondda and the valleys to the east slowly revert to nature, although the Usk valley escaped and maintains a pleasing landscape of hedged fields dotted with trees. Another strip of industry lies along the south coast between Newport and Swansea. From here westwards the countryside opens out again, reaching into the Gower, which remained one of the most culturally distinct parts of Wales into the early twentieth century. And then there is Pembroke, 'little England beyond Wales', settled with English in Henry VIII's reign, and still showing the legacy in English place names.

Given the mountainous landscape and the high rainfall it is inevitable that grazing sheep and cattle is a major occupation. The native sheep are small and hardy, black-woolled or with striped 'badger' faces; Welsh cattle are also

(previous page) The dramatic landscape of the Carneddau estate in Gwynedd. The peak on the left is Tryfan, a training ground for the first successful climbers of Everest. (above) An old apple tree at Llanerchaeron, Ceredigion.

black. Although there is a cheese named for the town of Caerphilly, making it ceased to be a Welsh concern for part of the twentieth century when production moved to the Somerset area. The recent revival of cheesemaking has affected Wales as much as England, and Caerphilly is now made in the area again; a number of other new-wave cheesemakers work further west, especially in the Pembrokeshire area. Cheese is popular; it is said that the slightly soft, moist texture of Caerphilly evolved to suit the tastes of coal miners, who used it in their packed meals. Welsh rarebits and other dishes involving cooked cheese are also widespread. Butter has long been an important dairy product in Wales; both Welsh butter and Welsh bacon are noted for being very salty.

West Wales, especially the level, fertile fields which

chequerboard the Pembroke coast, grows good early potatoes. Leeks, which are one of the national symbols of the country, are used in cookery but attempts to make them into often very good dishes in their own right seem slightly self-conscious, rather than rooted in firm tradition. The south-eastern part of Wales shares the cider and apple tradition, but otherwise fruit was grown only for local or domestic use.

Welsh cookery involves several techniques which are either unique to the country or have been forgotten elsewhere in Britain; simple methods of producing satisfying meals with the ingredients to hand and little more than an open fireplace to cook on. Broths and soups involving many ingredients are typical. The basic dish, *cawl*, involves two types of meat and numerous vegetables to provide broth and a main course from the same pot. Another unusual feature is the *planc*, the Welsh version of the griddle, which originally was a flat piece of iron balanced over an open fire. Electrically heated versions can be seen in action in Swansea market, especially for Welshcakes. But the *planc* was used for numerous other things – pancakes and pikelets, relatively large loaves made from conventional bread dough, and pastry turnovers filled with fruit, the sugar added after cooking to prevent the juices bubbling out. Until the early twentieth century oats were an important cereal in Wales, as in other upland areas of Britain, but the habit of using them to make oatcakes, dumplings, flummery and various drinks seems to have vanished.

(top) Golden tidal patterns at Red Wharf Bay, Anglesey.
(bottom) Sheep grazing peacefully in the grounds of Chirk Castle, Clwyd.

(above) Sheep being rounded up in the snowy Brecon Beacons, Powys.

WELSH LAMB, MUTTON AND LAVER

Welsh lamb and mutton has been praised for their flavour since the seventeenth century. In the mid-nineteenth century, George Borrow, the author of *Wild Wales*, remarked how he dined on an exquisite leg of mutton from the herb-scented pastures of the Berwyn in the 1830s. Now, a co-operative originally established by six National Trust tenants in Snowdonia markets both lamb and beef under the name Taste of Snowdonia. Meat is available from both Welsh mountain sheep and cross-breeds produced from the mountain flocks which graze on lower ground. Pure-bred Welsh mountain lamb is distinguished by its smaller size and, many would say, excellent flavour.

Salting mutton legs to produce 'hams' was recorded in several parts of Wales in the past, but no one appears to do this any longer. Relatively few wet-cooked dishes are recorded for it, although it was sometimes used in *cawl*, the soup-like stew which exists in numerous varieties in Wales. Roasting seems to have been the favoured method by all who could afford it. Sometimes the joint was wrapped in a huff paste of flour and water to protect it and retain the juices during cooking (a method recorded in Radnor).

To make a huff paste roast, you need a small, lean leg of well-flavoured Radnor lamb; make a firm paste with flour and water, season the leg and wrap it in the paste. Bake at 180°C/350°F/gas mark 4 for about 2 hours. Break off the crust and serve the meat with onion sauce . Alternatively, a small shoulder of lamb can be cooked on top of *tiesen nionod*, potato and onion baked together, (see page 200).

Roast lamb or mutton is also good with the south Welsh speciality laver, gathered from the Glamorgan and Pembroke coasts, and prepared by long, gentle cooking.

LAVER SAUCE

Laver is sold in local markets, it looks rather unpromising, a dark-brown sludge, but it makes an excellent sauce.

- 450g/1lb prepared laver
- 80g/3oz butter
- juice of 1 Seville orange
- salt and pepper

Heat the laver gently with the butter and season to taste with salt, pepper and orange juice. If Seville oranges are not in season, use lemon or tangerine juice. Serve very hot.

ONION SAUCE

This sauce is a traditional accompaniment for hot salt duck (see page 203), roast lamb or mutton.

Serves 4–6

- 2 large onions, peeled and sliced
- 150ml/5fl oz milk
- 25g/1oz butter
- 1 tablespoon plain flour
- salt, pepper and a little sugar
- 2–3 tablespoons double cream

Put the onions and milk in a pan with a little of the butter and cook very gently until the onions are almost a purée. In a separate pan, melt the rest of the butter and add the flour. Stir in the onion purée and bring to the boil. Season, adding a dust of sugar if the onions seem to lack sweetness, and stir in the cream.

CAWL

Similar to a gratin and good with a roast of
Welsh lamb.

Cawl is a stew-like soup made with lots of
vegetables and cheap cuts of meat, such as
boiling bacon, ham hock or beef brisket. It
was the all-purpose everyday dish of Welsh
farming communities, and everybody had
their own version. It's also impossible to make
quickly or in small quantities, but if you want
to feed a lot of people on a cold day it is ideal.
This recipe is adapted from one used by Bobby
Freeman. Like most dishes of this type, it
improves with re-heating.

Serves 4

- 900g/2lb potatoes, preferably a waxy variety such as
  'Desirée', peeled and thinly sliced
- 400g/14oz onions, peeled and chopped
- salt and pepper
- 75–100g/2¾–3½oz butter, plus extra for greasing

Serves 8

For the first stage
- 2 onions
- 2–3 large carrots
- 2 parsnips
- 1 medium swede or turnip

- beef dripping, bacon fat or oil
- 500–750g/1lb 2oz–1lb 10oz beef brisket
- 500–750g/1lb 2oz–1lb 10oz boiling bacon,
  or a ham hock
- 2 stalks of celery
- 1 bouquet garni
- pepper

Butter the inside of a baking dish or deep cake tin. Arrange
a layer of potato slices over the base, then add a layer of
onion, more potatoes, and so on until all the vegetables
are used. Season the layers with salt and pepper, dot with
butter and finish with potato. Cover with foil, pressing the
vegetables down well and bake at 180°C/350°F/gas mark 4.
The cake will cook in about an hour in a hot oven, or 1½
hours in a more moderate one.

A small joint of lamb can be cooked on top of the cake,
in which case, reduce the amount of butter involved to
about 25g/1oz and add a little stock.

For the second stage
- 500g/1lb 2oz small, new potatoes, scraped
- ½ small white cabbage, finely chopped
- 2–3 leeks, thinly sliced
- salt, pepper, chopped parsley

A very large pan or stockpot

Prepare all the root vegetables, except the potatoes, by
peeling and cutting them in rough cubes 2cm/¾in sq.
Chop the celery.

Melt the fat and brown the beef and ham or bacon, and
transfer it to the pan in which you intend to cook the *cawl*.
Next brown the root vegetables and add them to the meat.
Add the celery and enough cold water to cover. Bring to the
boil, skim, and add the bouquet garni and some pepper (no
salt at this stage). Simmer for about 4 hours. At this point,
the soup can be cooled and stored overnight if you wish.

For the second stage, remove the meat and carve into neat
squares, trimming off any fat and gristle. Return to the
soup along with the potatoes and simmer for a further 20
minutes. Taste and add salt and pepper as necessary. About
10 minutes before serving add the cabbage, then the leeks.
Serve in deep bowls, making sure each one gets a few slices
of meat. Sprinkle with chopped parsley.

(above) Moorland and a patchwork of fields overlooking the sea at Pen-y-Cil,
Gwynedd.

VALERIE BURKE'S ORCHARD PICNIC LOAF

Sometimes there just isn't enough time to do everything, which is how Mrs Burke made the sausage roll filling into a meatloaf one day. The fruit included is in celebration of the orchard at her farm in Pembrokeshire.

- 2 eggs, beaten
- 1 tablespoon of fresh herbs, chopped
- salt and pepper
- 1 teaspoon English mustard
- 750g/1lb 10oz good-quality pork sausage meat
- 1 onion, peeled and finely chopped
- 1 cooking apple, chopped
- 1 pear, chopped

A 900g/2lb loaf tin, lightly greased

Beat the eggs in a large mixing bowl. Stir in all the herbs and seasonings. Add the sausage meat and mix well with a fork or clean hands. Stir in the onion, apple and pear.

Place the mixture in the loaf tin and bake at 190°C/375°F/gas mark 5 for 50–60 minutes. Cool, turn out onto a dish and serve sliced with a watercress salad.

SALT DUCK

Although the early recipe for this suggests serving it hot with onion sauce, it is also delicious cold, carved thinly and served with a salad of oranges.

Serves 4

- 1 duck
- 100g/3½oz salt

Rub the duck all over with salt and put in a deep dish or other non-reactive container. Store in a cool place. Turn and rub the salt in twice a day for 3 days.

To cook, rinse off the excess salt and cover the duck with cold water. Simmer very gently for 2 hours. Serve hot or cold as desired.

FFAGOD

Or, faggots - one way of dealing with some of the less glamorous bits of pig, typical of South Wales and south-west England. Caul is a thin membrane with a lacy pattern of fat, which lines the stomach cavity of the animal; it wraps the mixture neatly, adds flavour and looks pretty. This recipe is from Glamorgan, and like many Welsh variants uses only liver and includes apple.

Serves 4

- 200g/7oz onion, peeled and cut in chunks
- 200g/7oz cooking apple, peeled and cored
- 200g/7oz pig's liver, cut in chunks
- 200g/7oz breadcrumbs
- 50g/1¾oz suet
- 20 sage leaves, shredded
- 1 teaspoon salt and some pepper
- 1 pig's caul
- stock

Mince or process the onion, apple and pig liver. Mix with the breadcrumbs, suet, sage, salt and pepper. Soak the caul in a bowl of warm water. After a few minutes it should be soft and easy to spread out. Using scissors cut 12 neat squares from it, avoiding the fattest bits. Divide the liver mixture into 12 and wrap each in a piece of the caul. Place in a greased ovenproof dish and add a little stock. Bake at 180°/350°F/gas mark 4 for about an hour.

BARLEY BREAD

A close-textured bread devised by Bobby Freeman, using the traditional Welsh staple of barley flour. Barley lacks gluten, so this bread will not rise like a conventional loaf.

- 1 scant tablespoon dried yeast
- 2 teaspoons molasses, sugar or honey
- 300ml/10fl oz tepid water
- 500g/1lb 2oz barley flour
- 1 scant tablespoon vegetable oil
- 1 dessertspoon salt

A 900g/2lb loaf tin, lightly greased

Cream the yeast with the molasses, sugar or honey and a little of the warm water. When it forms a frothy head, pour it into a bowl with the barley flour, oil and salt. Mix, adding more water to form a coherent but not sticky dough. Knead it for a few minutes, then leave in a warm place to rise for about 1 1/2 hours. Knock back, knead again, and place in the loaf tin. Prove for an hour. Make a deep cut along the top of the loaf and open out a little with your hand. Bake for an hour at 220°C/425°F/gas mark 7. Cool on a wire rack.

BROAD BEAN *CAWL*

This pretty pink and green soup is based on a harvest-time version of *cawl*. A busy farmer's wife would probably not bother to remove the pale outer skins of the beans, but it is worth the effort.

Serves 4

- 100–120g/3 1/2–4oz salty bacon, cut into matchsticks
- 200g/7oz new potatoes, scraped and cut into 1cm/1/2 in dice
- 1 small white turnip, peeled and cut into 1cm/1/2in dice
- 2 leeks (the white part only), sliced
- 850ml/1 1/2 pints water
- 1 dessertspoon fine oatmeal
- 200g/7oz broad beans (after podding) peeled of the greyish skin which clings to the bean
- 2 tablespoons fresh parsley, chopped
- salt and pepper
- Cheshire cheese, grated (optional)

Cook the bacon gently in the bottom of the soup pan, just until the fat begins to run. Add the potatoes, turnip, leeks and the water. Simmer gently until the vegetables are soft. Stir in the oatmeal, then add the broad beans and parsley. Cook for about 10 minutes more. Check the seasoning and serve in deep bowls. Some grated Cheshire cheese can be added to top each bowlful.

MRS ELLIS'S SHEARING CAKE

Mrs Ellis makes this cake every year at sheep-shearing time. She says 'It was handed down to me from my mother and my grandmother, and it has also been put in Katherine Hepburn's *Stories of My Life*. She was filming at our farm in *The Corn is Green* and they were doing the tea party scene in the garden and wanted a cake. I was asked if I had a cake, and I gave them my shearing cake, as we were going to shear the sheep the next day. They took it, but ate the lot and I had to make another one. The following day, Katherine Hepburn came to chat, as she often did because she was using our spare bedroom to change her clothes, and she asked if she could have the recipe for the cake as she enjoyed it so much. I wrote it down for her and blow me it was in her book!'

- 330g/11 ¹/₂ oz butter
- 450g/1lb self-raising flour
- 330g/11 ¹/₂ oz currants
- 330g/11 ¹/₂ oz caster sugar
- 2 eggs
- 200ml/7fl oz milk
- 1 tablespoon soft brown sugar

A 22cm/9in cake tin, well greased and lined

Rub the fat into the flour. Stir in the rest of the dry ingredients. Add the eggs and milk and stir well to make a soft, but not runny mixture. Place in the cake tin. Sprinkle the top of the cake with the brown sugar.

Bake at 200°C/400°F/gas mark 6 for 15 minutes, then reduce the heat to 170°C/325°F/gas mark 3 and bake for another 1 ³/₄ hours. Test with a skewer – when the cake is cooked it will come out clean. Cool in the tin.

WELSH RAREBIT

There are at least three basic versions of this toasted cheese dish. This is one of the more elaborate ones.

Serves 4

- 200g/7oz strong cheese, Cheddar or a good Cheshire, grated
- 25g/1oz butter
- 1 level teaspoon dry mustard
- 2 teaspoons plain flour
- 4 tablespoons beer
- pepper
- 4 slices of bread, toasted on one side

Put everything except the bread in a saucepan. Stir well and heat gently until all is melted and well amalgamated. Spread over the untoasted side of the bread and brown under the grill.

LITTLE CHEESE PUDDINGS

A bit like a baked Welsh rarebit, adapted from a much heftier recipe given by Bobby Freeman.

Serves 6 as a light lunch

- 6 thin slices white bread, crusts removed
- butter, for spreading and greasing
- 120g/4oz Cheddar cheese, grated
- 180ml/6 ¹/₂ fl oz single cream
- ¹/₂ teaspoon dry mustard
- pepper, a pinch of cayenne and a grate of nutmeg
- 5 eggs, beaten

6 individual ovenproof ramekins, buttered

Toast the bread on one side. Butter the untoasted side. Line each ramekin with a slice, toasted side down. Divide the cheese between the dishes. Bring the cream to the boil, add the seasonings and spices and beat in the eggs. Pour over the bread and cheese. Rest for 30 minutes, then bake at 190°C/375°F/gas mark 5 for 20–25 minutes, until well-risen and light brown. Serve immediately with a salad of watercress or bitter leaves.

SNOWDON PUDDING

A recipe which appears in all books on Welsh cookery; its connection to Wales is that in the nineteenth century it was served in a hotel at the foot of Mt Snowdon. It's also very good.

Serves 6–8

- 25g/1oz butter
- 75g/2³/₄oz good-quality raisins
- 250g/9oz suet
- 250g/9oz fine white breadcrumbs
- 40g/1¹/₂oz rice flour or cornflour
- pinch salt
- 140g soft light brown sugar
- 140g/5oz lemon marmalade
  (orange marmalade can be used instead)
- 6 eggs
- grated rinds of 2 lemons

A 1.2-litre/2-pint pudding basin, lavishly buttered

Divide the raisins but don't cut them completely in two. Use them to make a pattern round the inside of the basin, sticking them cut side to the butter. Mix the dry ingredients and marmalade. Beat the eggs well and stir in. Put the mixture in the basin, cover with foil or greaseproof paper, tie, and lower into a pan of boiling water. Boil for 1 hour and 15 minutes.

SHERRY OR MADEIRA SAUCE

- zest of ¹/₂ lemon, removed in thin pieces with a potato peeler
- 25g/1oz granulated sugar
- 150ml/5fl oz water
- 2 level teaspoons plain flour
- 25g/1oz butter
- 75ml/3fl oz sherry or Madeira

Simmer the lemon zest and sugar in the water for 10 minutes. Remove and discard the zest. Mix the flour and butter together over the heat and add to the lemon-flavoured syrup. Heat gently to thicken and add the sherry or Madeira.

SPICED PLUM TART

A Pembrokeshire farmer's wife contributed this recipe to *Farmhouse Fare* in the 1940s.

Serves 6–8

- 250g/9oz plain flour
- 40g/1¹/₂oz icing sugar
- ¹/₂ teaspoon cinnamon
- pinch of mixed spice
- pinch of salt
- 120g/4oz butter
- water to mix
- 450g/1lb plums, halved and stoned
- 4 small apples, peeled and cored
- 200g/7oz sugar
- beaten egg or milk to glaze

Mix the flour, icing sugar, cinnamon, spice and salt in a bowl. Rub in the butter and add enough water to make a stiffish dough.

Roll out two-thirds of the pastry and use it to line a pie dish. Add the plums, apples and sugar. Use the remaining pastry to cover and seal the pie. Glaze the pastry with beaten egg or milk. Bake at 200°C/400°F/gas mark 6 for 20 minutes, then lower the heat to 180°C/350°F/gas mark 4 and cook for another 20–25 minutes. Serve hot or cold.

Snowy view into the Ogwen Valley, Gwynedd.

Also known as *leicecs* or lightcakes, and relatives of crumpets, these were a tea-time tradition for guests in parts of north and central Wales. They'd be good for breakfast or brunch. Simple and very delicious.

'Speckled bread', another variation of the fruit bread theme so common in Britain. There are numerous minor variations but, like the Snowdon pudding recipe, it works better with really good raisins.

Makes 18

- 100g/3¹/₂ oz plain flour
- 45g/1¹/₂ oz caster sugar
- pinch of salt
- 60g/2¹/₂ oz sour cream or plain yoghurt
- 1 egg
- 100ml/3¹/₂ fl oz milk or buttermilk, if available
- lard or fat for greasing
- 1 teaspoon cream of tartar
- 1 teaspoon bicarbonate of soda
- salty butter to serve

Makes 2 loaves

- 100ml/3¹/₂ fl oz milk
- 1 teaspoon granulated sugar
- 1 scant tablespoon yeast
- 500g/1lb 2oz strong plain flour
- 120g/4oz soft brown sugar
- ¹/₂ teaspoon salt
- ¹/₂ teaspoon mixed spice
- 120g/4oz lard or butter, or a mixture of both
- 175g/6oz good-quality raisins
- 175g/6oz currants
- 50g/1³/₄ oz mixed candied peel, chopped
- 1 egg

Mix the flour, sugar and salt in a small bowl. Add the sour cream or yoghurt and begin to mix. Break in the egg and stir vigorously to make a smooth batter. Blend in the milk. You should have a batter which drops nicely off the spoon. This much can be done in advance.

Just before cooking, set a griddle to heat (a heavy frying pan will do, but a griddle is much easier), or use the hotplate if your cooker has one. It needs to be quite hot and well greased.

Mix the cream of tartar and bicarbonate of soda in a small bowl and add a tablespoon of water. Immediately pour the mixture into the batter and stir well.

Drop in tablespoons on the hot griddle. When the underside is golden and the top full of little holes, flip each cake over with a spatula and cook for a moment on the other side.

Serve immediately with butter.

Two 1.2-litre/2-pint loaf tins, greased

Warm the milk, add a pinch of sugar and the yeast. Mix the flour, sugar, salt and spice, and rub in the fat roughly. Stir in the dried fruit and peel. Add the yeast mixture and the egg and mix to a dough, adding a little more water or milk if necessary. Knead well, then allow to rise until doubled in size, this may take 2 hours. Knock back, divide into 2 pieces and shape each into a loaf. Place in the loaf tins and prove until well risen. Bake at 200°C/400°F/gas mark 6 for 15 minutes, then lower the heat to 180°C/350°F/gas mark 4 and cook for a further 40–45 minutes, or until the loaves sound hollow when tapped underneath. Best kept a couple of days before cutting. Serve buttered.

GINGERBREAD

A very good recipe collected in central Wales in the 1930s. The use of sour cream and the mixture of spices seem more Germanic or North American than British, but many households, farms included, acquired recipes from elsewhere via friends or family who had gone into service, or migrated to the colonies and sent home novel recipes.

- 120g/4oz butter
- 120g/4oz caster sugar
- 80g/3oz golden syrup
- 1 whole egg and 1 egg white
- 1 teaspoon bicarbonate of soda
- 120g/4oz raisins
- 60g/2oz mixed candied peel, chopped
- 75ml/3fl oz sour cream
- 250g/9oz plain flour
- 1 teaspoon baking powder
- $^1/_2$ teaspoon ground ginger
- $^1/_2$ teaspoon ground cinnamon
- $^1/_2$ teaspoon ground cloves

A 22cm/8$^1/_2$ in shallow square cake tin

Cream the butter and sugar together. Warm the syrup and beat into the mixture. Separate the egg and mix in the yolk. Mix the bicarbonate of soda with a tablespoon of boiling water and stir in. Add the raisins, peel and sour cream, and mix in the flour, baking powder and spices. Whisk the egg whites to a stiff froth and fold in, making sure everything is well mixed. Put the mixture in the cake tin and bake at 170°C/325°F/gas mark 3 for 1 $^1/_4$–1 $^1/_2$ hours. Turn onto a cake rack to cool and store in a tin.

CYFLAITH (WELSH TOFFEE)

Toffee-pulls, in which family and friends would gather in an evening to make toffee, may be a thing of the past, but making toffee and other simple sweets was often an activity of farmhouse kitchens.

- 500g/1lb 2oz black treacle
- 500g/1lb 2oz Demerara sugar
- 120g/4oz butter
- 1 teaspoon vinegar

A marble slab or large tray for working the mixture

Put all the ingredients in a large saucepan. Heat over a low flame, stirring to ensure all the sugar melts. Once it has dissolved, increase the heat and boil fairly briskly. After 10 minutes, test by dropping a teaspoon of mixture into cold water. If it hardens at once, the mixture is ready. Pour it immediately onto the slab or tray.

Butter both hands and (cautiously) begin to pull the mixture into strands. Initially, it will be very hot and, whilst a skin forms on the surface, the centre retains its heat more. As it cools, you should be able to fold and stretch the mixture more intensively, giving long golden strands of toffee. Cut into small pieces whilst still warm and store in an airtight container.

BLACKBERRY CURD

A delicious preserve based on the same principle as lemon curd (see page 163).

- 500g/1lb 2oz blackberries
- 150g/5 $^1/_2$ oz apple, peeled and cored
- juice of 1 lemon
- 600g/1lb 7oz granulated sugar
- 100g/3 $^1/_2$ oz unsalted butter
- 3 eggs, beaten

Simmer the blackberries and the peeled, cored apple in just enough water to cover until soft. Sieve and put the juice in a double boiler. Add the lemon juice, sugar and butter and stir over heat until the sugar dissolves. Beat the eggs and stir these in. Cook gently until the mixture thickens. Pot in warm sterilised jars and store in the fridge. Eat within 6 weeks.

Farmland near Dolgellau in the Snowdonia National Park, Gwent.

There are two words everyone associates with the Irish countryside, green and damp. The green comes in many shades – yellowish, for a new-mown hay meadow, emerald for the pastures, deep viridian for late summer trees and hedges. There are other colours too – the black and white of basalt and chalk at the Giant's Causeway, the wine of heather in bloom, the brilliant acid-yellow of gorse in flower, smoky blues of mountains in the distance and of loughs reflecting the sky, which may be anything from the palest limpid blue to lowering steel-grey. As for the damp, that's what keeps the landscape green.

The province of Northern Ireland is the most north-eastern part of Ireland, a rough circle from Belfast round through the clear waters and green islets of Strangford Lough, past the mountains of Mourne to Newry. From here the border with Southern Ireland winds inland to the west to take in Upper and Lower Lough Erne, and then returns northwards to Londonderry. The scenery of the northern coast is spectacularly beautiful, with the Glens of Antrim and on the coast the Giant's Causeway, offering a particularly pleasing combination of land and water, with flat green fields divided by walls. Inland are the heather and tawny grass of the Sperrin mountains and the expanse of Lough Neagh. To the south of this Counties Tyrone and Armagh provide lush arable farmland. The prevailing westerly winds bring rain only, no pollution, and waterways and the air are very clean.

Northern Irish food, whilst obviously related to that of mainland Britain, has its own characteristics. The greenness of the countryside is reflected in the grass-fed beef and lamb from the Antrim hills and the Sperrin mountains. The beef is reared with particular care, and

(previous page) Ardkeen on the eastern side of Strangford Lough, Co Down.
(above) Dark clouds above the Mourne mountains, Co Down. Slieve Donard, the highest peak in Northern Ireland is in the distance.

farmers in Northern Ireland introduced a traceability scheme to assure quality and safety well before those on the UK mainland. Pork is eaten, fresh or as ham or bacon, in a piece, or in rashers, as part of the 'Ulster fry', the Northern Irish version of the cooked breakfast. There is also a strong tradition of hunting and eating game – pheasants, pigeons, venison and, for those lucky enough to live in the south-westernmost corner, snipe. Fish, both from the sea and from inland waters, is an essential part of the diet.

Armagh is Northern Ireland's orchard county, producing apples and strawberries. Making jams and chutneys is part of the tradition of domestic cookery. A limited selection of good vegetables, especially root crops, are grown and used in the kitchen. Potatoes are by far the most important, and the Irish kitchen as a whole includes a remarkable variety of potato dishes. They do well in the mild damp climate as, sadly, does potato blight, which precipitated the disastrous famine of the 1840s.

The other great products of the land are butter and the buttermilk left over from churning. Butter is used for frying, baking, on bread and mixed into potatoes. Buttermilk gives a unique touch to several Irish breads and potato dishes, and really is essential for texture and especially flavour. If you can't get the real thing an approximation – no more – can be made by thinning a little Greek yoghurt with milk and adding a spoonful of sour cream to give a mixture with a texture resembling single cream. With such an emphasis on butter, cheese has never been very important, although some Irish farmers,

like their counterparts in Britain, have worked creatively with continental traditions of cheesemaking.

The home-baking tradition, both for bread and fancier items, is alive and well. Bread is routinely made at home. Yeast is now not used in Northern Irish baking, but soda bread and wheaten (wholemeal) bread raised with bicarbonate of soda and buttermilk or cream of tartar are well known outside the territory. Apart from buttermilk, a particular type of flour is needed to make soda bread well, and this is difficult to buy outside Ireland; to make wheaten bread, look for a low-protein, coarse-ground, wholemeal flour, and avoid soda bread 'mixes'.

LMS NORTHERN IRELAND
by Hesketh Hubbard V-P.R.B.A.R.O.I.

(top) Columns of basalt rock, known as 'the Organ' at Giant's Causeway, Co Antrim.
(bottom) A London Midland Scottish Railway poster of 1944 showing a lush and green Irish countryside.

BEEF, GUINNESS AND OYSTER PIE

IRISH STEW

The oysters are a subtle addition to this rich and hearty pie. Oysters can be tricky to open - so if you're nervous, ask your fishmonger to do it for you.

Serves 6

- 50g/1 ¾ oz dripping or oil
- 1 large onion, peeled and chopped
- 2 garlic cloves, crushed
- 4 tablespoons plain flour
- 1 teaspoon salt and some pepper
- 750g/1lb 10oz stewing beef, trimmed of all fat and gristle and cut into large cubes
- 400ml/14fl oz beef stock
- 300ml/10fl oz Guinness
- 1 tablespoon fresh, chopped thyme
- 1 tablespoon fresh, chopped parsley
- 12 oysters
- 500g/1lb 2oz puff pastry
- 1 egg, beaten for glazing

Heat the dripping or oil in a casserole. Add the onions and garlic and fry gently until soft, for around 20 minutes. Remove with a slotted spoon and put on one side. Mix the flour, salt and pepper and toss the beef in it. Brown it in the fat left over from frying the onions. Shake in any leftover flour and stir to absorb the fat. Return the onions to the pan and add the beef stock and the Guinness, stirring well. Add the parsley and thyme, cover and transfer to a low oven 150°C/300°F/gas mark 2 for 2 ½–3 hours. When cooked, pour the mixture into a deep pie dish and allow to cool.

Just before cooking, open the oysters and add the flesh and any juices (strained) to the beef mixture. Roll out the pastry to 5mm/ ¼ in thickness and cover the pie. Cut leaves or other decorations for the top from scraps, and glaze over the pastry with beaten egg.

Bake at 220°C/350°F/gas mark 7 for 20 minutes, then reduce the heat to 180°C/350°F/gas mark 4 and bake for a further 30 minutes.

This is a simple dish, but even so it has many variants. Does one add carrots or not? Is it better with or without pearl barley? Should half the potatoes be sliced and added at the start of cooking, to thicken the stew, and the others left whole and added with just enough time to cook at the end? It is one of those dishes with a formula, rather than a recipe, and this one uses twice as much potato by weight as meat, half as much onion, and not too much liquid.

Serves 6

- 1kg/2 ¼ lb best end or middle neck of lamb or mutton, cut into chops
- 2kg/4 ½ lb potatoes, peeled and sliced about 1cm/ ½ in thick
- 500g onion, peeled, thinly sliced and roughly chopped
- salt and pepper
- 1 tablespoon fresh, chopped thyme
- 1 tablespoon mushroom ketchup (optional)
- 200ml/7fl oz water or stock

Layer the ingredients in a deep casserole, starting with the meat, adding onion and then potato. Sprinkle over the seasonings, and repeat, finishing with potato. Add a little water or stock and bring to the boil. Cover tightly, and transfer to the oven pre-heated to 180°C/350°F/gas mark 4 for 2–2 ½ hours. Check from time to time to ensure that it is not drying up, and add a little more liquid if necessary. The longer and slower the cooking the better, and the stew re-heats well.

ULSTER BROTH

A 'visiting' dish, always on the simmer at midday for whoever's around or in the evening for when the family returns home. 'Soup celery' is dried celery leaves; use the leaves from the centre of a head of celery if you can't buy this. 'Soup mix' is a mixture of pearl barley, split peas and red lentils, sold in Northern Ireland and some parts of mainland Britain. If you can't buy this, use a third of each of the pulses to make up the weight given below.

Serves 6

- 2 litres/3 $^1/_2$ pints good chicken or beef stock
- 1 large onion, chopped fairly finely
- soup celery or 1 handful of celery leaves
- 2 large carrots, peeled and chopped
- 1 handful of fresh parsley, chopped
- 120g/4oz soup mix or mixed pulses, (pearl barley, split peas and red lentils)
- salt and pepper
- fresh parsley to serve

Put the stock in a large pan and set over the heat. Add the onion, celery leaves, carrots, chopped parsley and soup mix or pulses, plus a teaspoon of salt and simmer gently for about an hour. By this time the pulses should be cooked. Taste, add more salt and pepper as required and serve with a little fresh, chopped parsley in each bowlful. This is one of those dishes which tastes even better re-heated the next day. A bowl of this soup with a good slice of wheaten bread is a complete meal.

CHAMP

Comfort food. The standard version uses spring onions; if you're being posh, use chives instead. Serve with boiled bacon, sliced off the piece, and boiled cabbage.

Serves 2

- 500–600g/1lb 2oz–1lb 5oz potatoes
- salt and pepper
- 100ml/3 $^1/_2$ oz buttermilk
- handful of chives or 6 spring onions
- butter, to serve

Peel the potatoes, cut in suitable chunks and boil until tender. Drain, season with salt and pepper and mash with the buttermilk. For an onion or chive version, chop the greenery into short lengths, add to the buttermilk and warm until almost boiling. Beat the mixture into the mashed potato. Serve very hot in individual portions, each shaped into a mound with a hollow containing a piece of butter in the middle.

OATMEAL HERRING AND NETTLE CHAMP

I am indebted to Fionnuala Jay O'Boyle at Taste of Ulster for this idea. Her grandmother used to make this for tea. It is well worth trying, a delicious combination of textures and flavours.

Serves 2

- $^1/_2$ teaspoon salt
- 15g/ $^1/_2$ oz fine oatmeal
- 2 fresh herrings, cleaned, but with the heads on (use filleted herring if you prefer)
- 2 handfuls young nettles, washed, blanched and coarsely chopped
- 25g/1oz butter for frying

Mix the salt with the oatmeal and coat the herring with it. Melt the butter in a frying pan and fry the herring over a low heat. Whole herrings will need cooking around 5 minutes per side, fillets will take 3 minutes per side. The skin should be beautifully brown and crisp.

Serve with nettle champ by following the champ recipe (see above), and substituting nettles for the onions or chives.

(above) A Lockheed Hudson flying over the Northern Irish countryside in 1941. The photograph was taken to demonstrate the plane's effective camouflage. (right) The abandoned settlement of Crocknanagh on Rathlin Island, Co Antrim.

STUFFED PORK FILLET

A 1920s recipe, collected by Florence White.

Serves 4

- 600–700g/1lb 5oz–1 ½ lb pork fillet

For the stuffing
- 60g/2oz onion, finely chopped
- 25g/1oz butter
- 120g/4oz fresh white breadcrumbs
- 3 teaspoons fresh sage, chopped
- 3 teaspoons fresh parsley, chopped
- salt and pepper
- milk to mix
- butter, for the dish
- plain flour, for the gravy
- stock, wine or water, for the gravy

To make the stuffing, cook the onion gently in the butter. Mix it with the breadcrumbs and herbs and season with salt and pepper. Bind with milk.

Cut the pork fillet obliquely to give thin slices. If these don't seem to have a very large surface area, put them between sheets of baking parchment and beat them out a little with a rolling pin or cutlet bat. Divide the stuffing between them, and roll each slice up, securing the roll with a cocktail stick or tying with thread.

Butter an ovenproof dish which will hold the fillets nicely and place the rolls in it. Dust over with flour and dot with a little more butter. Cook at 200°C/400°F/gas mark 6 for 15–20 minutes.

Remove the cooked pork from the dish and keep warm. Add a little more butter to the cooking residues in the pan, and a dusting of flour. Deglaze with stock, wine or water to make a little gravy. Serve with mashed potatoes and apple sauce.

WHEATEN BREAD

Quick and easy to make, this is best made with wholemeal flour with a relatively low protein content. This is easy to buy in Ireland, but more difficult in mainland Britain. Nora Brown, in a leaflet about Ulster breads, suggests adding 25g/1oz oatmeal and 25g/1oz brown sugar, and gives an alternative method of baking, which is to put the dough in a tin greased heavily with butter to give a nice crust.

- 500g/1lb 2oz wholemeal flour, plus a little extra for dusting
- 1 teaspoon salt
- 1 teaspoon bicarbonate of soda
- 1 ½ teaspoons cream of tartar
- 400ml/14fl oz buttermilk

Mix the flour, salt and bicarbonate of soda in a bowl. Add the cream of tartar to the milk and stir this mixture into the dry ingredients. Mix quickly but thoroughly to make a slightly wet dough. Turn onto a well-floured surface and cut in half. Shape each piece into a round, cut a cross halfway through the top of each and place on a floured baking tray. Bake immediately at 200°C/400°F/gas mark 6 for 30–40 minutes. Soda bread goes stale quickly, so try to use it within 24 hours.

(left) A volunteer warden and Babe the pig on Bally Quintin Farm, Co Down. (above) Strangford Lough is one of Europe's most important wildlife sites. Flocks of wintering wildfowl can be seen here along with seals and otters.

BARM BRACK

SODA FARLS

With apologies to the contemporary Ulster baking tradition, which now relies on cream of tartar and bicarbonate of soda to raise breads and cakes of all kinds. This is a recipe which dates to 1825, before chemical raising agents were available. No apologies for the results, which are superb.

- 1 dessertspoon dried yeast
- 50ml/2fl oz warm water
- 500g/1lb 2oz plain flour
- 60g/2oz caster sugar
- 1 scant teaspoon salt
- 15g/$^{1}/_{2}$ oz caraway seeds
- 250ml/8 $^{1}/_{2}$ fl oz milk, hand hot
- 40g/1 $^{1}/_{2}$ oz butter plus a little for greasing
- 1 egg

A cake tin 20cm/8in in diameter

Set the yeast to work with a pinch of sugar and the warm water. Mix the flour, sugar, salt and seeds. Warm the milk to hand-hot and melt the butter in it. Beat in the egg. Mix this into the flour to make a dough, adding a little more milk or water if necessary. Knead well, place in a bowl and allow to rise in a warm place for 3 hours. Knock back, put into a greased cake tin and prove for about 40 minutes.

Bake at 200°C/400°F/gas mark 6 for 20 minutes, then lower the heat to 180°C/350°F/gas mark 4 and bake for a further 15–20 minutes. If the base of the cake sounds hollow when tapped, it is done. Turn out of the tin and cool on a wire rack. Excellent with butter and cheese.

Delicious for tea with butter and jam, or for breakfast with scrambled eggs, and maybe some smoked trout.

- 200g/7oz plain, unbleached white flour, plus extra for dusting
- 1 level teaspoon baking powder
- $^{1}/_{2}$ teaspoon salt
- 160ml/5$^{1}/_{2}$ fl oz buttermilk

An iron griddle or a large, heavy, clean frying pan for cooking

Sieve the flour, baking powder and salt into a bowl. Add the buttermilk and stir well to make a soft dough (you may need to add a little more liquid). Turn the dough onto a well-floured surface and work briefly to make sure everything is well mixed. The dough should be quite sticky. Pat out into a circle 1cm/$^{1}/_{2}$in thick.

Heat the griddle or frying pan gently. Sprinkle lightly with flour. When the flour begins to brown lightly, place the circle of dough onto it. Pat down lightly and cut into quarters. Cook gently and try not to let it scorch. After about 10 minutes, turn each quarter over in the pan; the cooked side should have golden-brown patches on it. Cook for a further 5–7 minutes. Serve straight away, with breakfast, or with butter and jam.

(above) Exotic introductions, like azaleas, mingle with native habitat at Rowallane Garden, Co Down.

POTATO AND APPLE CAKE

A variation on apple pie, from a 1920s recipe given by Florence White. Use Bramley apples grown in Armagh to give a taste of Ulster.

Serves 8

For the pastry
- 2 large potatoes, peeled and cut into chunks
- 250g/9oz plain flour
- salt
- 80g/3oz beef dripping or butter
- 1 egg yolk, plus 1 whole egg, beaten for glazing the pie
- 50ml/2fl oz milk

For the filling
- 1kg/2 ¼ lb apples, peeled, cored and sliced
- 175g/6oz Demerara sugar

A deep pie dish 20cm/8in in diameter

Boil the potatoes until tender. Mash well and allow to cool a little. Put the flour and a little salt in a bowl and grate in the dripping or butter. Mix well and add the potato and the egg yolk and keep mixing. It will make a soft dough; add a little milk if it seems on the dry side but try not to over mix. Divide into 3 portions, one slightly bigger; roll this one out and use to line the pie dish. Cover the base with half the apples and scatter in half the sugar. Roll out a second portion of dough and put over the apples; scatter the remaining apples on top of this and add the rest of the sugar. Roll out the third portion of dough and use it to cover the pie, sealing the edges. Glaze with the beaten egg.

Bake at 200°C/400°F/gas mark 6 for 20 minutes then turn the heat down to 180°C/350°F/gas mark 4 and continue to cook for 20–25 minutes, or until the pastry is golden-brown in patches. This is best eaten hot straight after baking as the pastry becomes very solid when cold, although it can be re-heated.

HAZELNUT CAKE

The crunch of the hazelnuts contrasts pleasingly with the raspberries in this light sponge.

- 3 large eggs, separated
- 150g/5 ½ oz caster sugar
- juice of ½ a lemon
- 60g/2oz hazelnuts, skin on, finely ground
- 30g/1 ¼ oz plain flour, sifted
- 100ml/3 ½ fl oz whipping cream, whipped to soft peaks
- 120g/4oz fresh raspberries

A loose-bottomed 20-cm/8-in cake tin, brushed with melted butter and dusted with caster sugar

Whisk the egg yolks and sugar together until thick and pale. Add the lemon juice. Fold in the nuts, then the flour. Whisk the egg whites until they hold a stiff peak. Stir a third of the whites into the hazelnut mixture to slacken it off, then gently fold in the remaining whites. Pour the mixture into the cake tin and bake at 180C/350F/gas mark 4 for 35–40 minutes. Cool in the tin. When cool, remove from the tin, carefully cut in half horizontally and fill with whipped cream and raspberries.

FARMING AND FOOD IN THE TWENTY-FIRST CENTURY

Food is an interface along which the rural and urban connect every day. However processed a food, the bulk of it will have been grown by someone, somewhere, on a piece of land (along with much else – fibres for textiles, building timber, biomass for fuel and the less tangible products of the leisure industry). It is only recently that the links between landscape and food production have been revived in the UK, and this has mostly been in the form of crisis management. February 2001 brought the news every livestock farmer dreads: a case of foot and mouth disease had been confirmed in the UK. The dynamics of the epidemic – spread largely through the movement of sheep by dealers – had a disproportionate effect on tenants of National Trust land, much of which is in areas in which sheep- and cattle-farming are predominant, and which were already suffering economically. Closure of footpaths, as well as the press coverage, which discouraged visitors to the British countryside, made things worse, as remote rural communities rely as much, or more, on tourism than they do on farming to provide income. All this at a time when the number of farmers and the overall contribution of farming to the economy is declining.

Many people consider that farming does not serve the environment well. A valid point, but they ignore a central truth which is that without farming, our landscapes – including the most beautiful, apparently natural ones – would lose their meaning and their means of management.

So what is being done to help the farming community resolve problems, and how can consumers, purchasing food, encourage environmentally friendly, sustainable agriculture? The problems of the countryside in general reflect larger changes – globalisation, changes in transport, packaging technology and retailing of food, poor rural infrastructure and a lack of affordable housing for the young. On an individual level, diversification is seen as the main way in which farmers can increase incomes whilst providing stewardship for the countryside. There are numerous initiatives centred on food which are aimed both at encouraging environmentally friendly farming techniques and more thoughtful consumption, with the overall objective of improving rural incomes and encouraging a high-quality environment. Schemes such as the National Trust's Plot to Plate project and the Countryside Agency's Eat the View campaign make this link explicit. Re-creating local food economies and re-establishing consumer confidence whilst encouraging a healthy diet that tastes good are also essential. These things do not, of course sit easily with the evolution of agriculture in this country over the last sixty years.

Encouraging local food economies is something that has received much attention over the past five years. The aims include reducing 'food miles' (the distance food travels to reach the consumer), raising awareness of local food production, and re-connecting the producer and consumer by direct marketing. In the growing number of farmers' markets across the country, local producers go to consumers. Many small- to medium- sized towns have established such markets over the past four or five years.

(top) Two Large Black Pigs at Bosigran Farm, Cornwall.
(bottom) A field planted with clover at Lower Sizergh Farm, Cumbria. The clover encourages nitrogen-rich soil.

By restricting access to those producers within a specified radius of the market the whole thing is kept local and seasonal and producers and consumers have an opportunity to meet and talk. Alternatively, consumers can go to producers by purchasing from farm shops. This gives the consumer more opportunity to put the production of food into context, by seeing the place in which their food is grown or reared. Farm shops which rely on produce grown on the farm can also offer guarantees of quality, especially for home-produced meat.

New, innovative forms of direct marketing include the 'vegetable box', in which market gardeners or farmers growing vegetables deliver a box of seasonal produce to the doorstep on a regular basis. Many farms now have websites with information about the farm and its produce, which can be ordered over the internet and is then delivered, suitably packaged, by post or courier. The idea of the retailer is not completely ignored however, and l ocal food shops are an important element in local food economies. Also, it has to be acknowledged that not all producers are willing or able to involve themselves in direct marketing, just as not all consumers are equipped to respond to the idea. Supermarkets are therefore unlikely to disappear in the near future and should be encouraged both to inform customers about how their purchasing decisions affect the well-being of the countryside, and source more local produce.

Local food economies can also be developed by encouraging local sourcing by hotels, bed-and-breakfasts and cafés, especially if they acknowledge this in their marketing. Food is a significant element in making a holiday enjoyable, and farms often run cafés or bed and breakfast facilities as part of their activities (one or two even run pubs or restaurants). The Heart of England Tourist Board runs an award scheme for restaurants that source their ingredients locally, display a mark and have a database to help people find them. The idea has also been developed into 'food trails' of local specialities, producers and retailers in places. The purchasing power of institutional catering is often overlooked, but the idea of local sourcing in this field is being encouraged by the government. Money spent in local food economies tends to remain in the community, as opposed to supermarkets, where only a little remains locally.

Establishing closer links between producers and consumers should go some way to restoring consumer confidence in food production. This loss of confidence has manifested itself in numerous ways over the past twenty years, including a trend away from meat-eating and several heavily reported 'food scandals' such as salmonella in egg production, BSE in beef and food poisoning incidents. Whilst farming methods have contributed to these, they are not the whole story. Agriculture is a complex business involving companies producing feed, fertilizers, herbicides and pesticides. It is a balance between human and mechanical labour, and changing farm subsidies. Crucially, farms do not control what happens to the food once it leaves their premises and

A basket of eggs for sale at Osterley Park Farm Shop, London.

is processed and cooked.

Producers can help consumers reach an informed decision about what to buy if they make the food's origins more transparent. One way is to improve traceability and to adopt recognised growing and welfare standards. Several schemes already exist, including the National Farmer's Union's Little Red Tractor, and the RSPCA's Freedom Food assurance schemes. In the past decade organic produce has become increasingly familiar to consumers. Organic certification provides an assurance of animal welfare and environmental standards, based on the principles of crop rotations and the avoidance of conventional agro-chemicals.

Whilst the organic sector has expanded over the last few years, it is recognised that conventional farming is likely to remain the major system in the UK for the foreseeable future. The National Trust would like to see the development of more robust environmental standards, based on the best practice of both conventional farming methods and organic techniques. These would be independently inspected and based on an appraisal of the whole farm, from both an environmental and business point of view. However, the input of farmers in terms of extra time and care required by these systems needs to be rewarded with genuine price premiums.

The development of regional brands can also help add value to primary produce. The idea of regionality received relatively little attention in the UK during the post-war period, when the emphasis was on producing bulk raw ingredients for purchasing boards. However, since the early 1990s interest in this has revived, partly through encouragement from the EU. Due to the anonymous nature of mass food production we have lost, forgotten or do not appreciate the special associations between foods and the places in which they are produced. This problem has been exacerbated by the lack of infrastructure associated with small-scale local food processing; during the foot and mouth epidemic, it became apparent that the closure of local abattoirs played a part in the spread of the disease, because it meant livestock was transported further before slaughter. There are welfare and food quality issues involved as well. Most farmers respect the animals they work with and do not wish them to undergo long and potentially traumatic journeys to slaughter, and any butcher will affirm that an animal which is relaxed and well rested at the point of slaughter provides better meat. The retention of such local facilities is necessary to maintain the advantages which can be lost in more economic centralised premises.

When it comes to producing finished products, farms may also face barriers. They often struggle to access food handling facilities for cutting meat or preparing food, and need financial and practical help in establishing them as knowledge of local traditional products has been heavily eroded. In addition, farmers may also need help with development ideas. One sector which has achieved notable success in this area is artisan cheesemaking, which went from being almost non-existent in the 1970s to become

(top) Ploughed fields of winter stubble at Southdown Farm, Devon.
(bottom) A farmer with his quad bike and sheepdog at Hill Top Farm, Cumbria.

a flourishing craft industry, although the knowledge is usually regarded as the intellectual property of an individual or a company rather than a community. Yet such developments must be welcomed because they create jobs, stimulate associated industries, and ensure wealth is created and retained in rural areas.

Developing local food economies, establishing assurance schemes and encouraging regional brands are all initiatives that need help at many levels. Some will come from within the farming community itself, using the skills and knowledge of older farmers. And on a wider level, local producer groups (a Taste of Ulster, Yorkshire Pantry, etc.) can contribute by providing publicity and information on companies within their area. National organisations such as the Countryside Agency and the National Trust also have a role.

Financial incentives, of course, play a large part. Historically, farmers have been rewarded via a subsidy system for producing as much as possible. In Britain, the Common Agricultural Policy tended to exacerbate this. It remains to be seen whether the reforms due to commence in 2005 will encourage a model of agriculture more sympathetic to the environment and the communities which work the land and encourage market-led production. The provision of free business and environmental planning advice is one place to begin.

The onus to change should not be completely on rural communities. Knowledgeable consumers are needed if choice is to be truly informed, and producers and consumers are to support each other. One suggestion is to give children a free farm visit to see for themselves what is involved in food production. Farmers are in fact already diversifying into education by providing visitor centres, information packs and guided walks, and using the idea of the countryside as an outdoor classroom, which is something the organic movement in particular is already exploring. Further up the education scale, an expansion of skills training in sustainable land management would help to provide a new generation of environmentally concerned farmers. It would, of course, be an advantage if their role in land stewardship was publicly acknowledged and rewarded, and their opinions sought and noted when decisions have to be made.

That change is necessary in farming is agreed. But it is the farmers who have to implement and live with the changes. The countryside is a complex living and working environment, not a museum which closes every evening when the visitors go home.

DRY MEASURES

1 US cup	50g	2oz of breadcrumbs
1 US cup	75g	$3^1/_2$oz of rolled oats
1 US cup	90g	$3^1/_2$oz of desiccated coconut
1 US cup	100g	$3^1/_2$oz of walnut pieces, icing sugar
1 US cup	120g	4oz of white flour
1 US cup	150g	$5^1/_2$oz of wholemeal flour
1 US cup	175g	6oz mixed peel, sultanas
1 US cup	200g	7oz Demerara sugar, rice
1 US cup	225g	$^1/_2$lb of cream cheese
1 US cup	300g	11oz of mincemeat
1 US cup	350g	12oz of treacle, jam

LIQUID MEASURES

$^1/_4$ US cup	60ml	2 fluid oz
1 US cup	240ml	8 fluid oz
2 US cups (1 US pint)	480ml	16 fluid oz

BUTTER, LARD AND MARGARINE MEASURES

$^1/_4$ stick	25g	2 level tablespoons	1oz
1 stick (1 US cup)	100g	8 level tablespoons	$3^1/_2$oz

BIBLIOGRAPHY

Lady Clark: *The Cookery Book of Lady Clark of Tillypronie*. Southover Press 1994

Farmer's Weekly: *Farmhouse Fare*, 1950

Theodora Fitzgibbon: *A Taste of Wales*. Pan, 1971

Theodora Fitzgibbon: *A Taste of the West Country*. Pan, 1972

Theodora Fitzgibbon: *A Taste of the Lake District*. Pan, 1980

Bobby Freeman: *First Catch Your Peacock*. Y Lolfa Cyfo, 1996

Jane Grigson: *English Food*. Penguin Books, 1992

Nell Heaton: *A Calendar of Country Receipts*. Faber and Faber, 1950

Nell Heaton: *Traditional Recipes of the British Isles*. Faber and Faber, 1951

Nell Heaton: *Nell Heaton's Cooking Dictionary*. Cresta Books, 1953

Sheila Hutchins: *Your Granny's Cook Book*. Daily Express, 1971

Mrs C. F. Leyel and Miss Olga Hartley: *The Gentle Art of Cookery*. Chatto and Windus, 1925

Sara Paston-Williams: *Jams, Preserves and Edible Gifts*. The National Trust, 1999.

S. Minwel Tibbott: *Welsh Fare*. National Museum of Wales, 1976

Alison Uttley: *Recipes From an Old Farmhouse*. Faber and Faber Ltd, 1966

Mrs Arthur Webb: *Farmhouse Cookery*. George Newnes and Sons, undated, *c.* 1930

Florence White: *Good Things in England*. Jonathan Cape, 1932

National Federation of Women's Institutes: *Traditional Fare of England and Wales*. 1948

West Kent Federation of Women's Institutes: *The Country Housewife's Handbook*. 1943

Yorkshire Federation of Women's Institutes: *Yorkshire Recipes*. 1937

USEFUL ADDRESSES

The National Farmer's Union
Agriculture House
164 Shaftesbury Avenue
London
WC2H 8HL
www.nfu.org.uk

RSPCA
Enquiries Service,
Wilberforce Way,
Southwater,
Horsham,
West Sussex
RH13 9RS
www.freedomfood.org

National Farmers' Retail & Markets Association (FARMA)
PO BOX 575
Southampton
SO15 7BZ
www.farmersmarkets.net

The National Trust
36 Queen Anne's Gate,
London
SW1H 9AS
www.nationaltrust.org.uk

PICTURE CREDITS

JACKET
National Trust Photographic Library/ John Hammond

INTRODUCTION
Page 6 National Trust Photographic Library/ Joe Cornish
Page 8 (top) National Trust Photographic Library (bottom) Beamish Museum
Page 9 Public Record Office
Page 10 National Trust Photographic Library/ Joe Cornish
Page 11 Heritage Image Partnership
Page 12 National Trust Photographic Library/ Ray Hallett
Page 13 Heritage Image Partnership

CORNWALL
Pages 14-15 National Trust Photographic Library/Paul Wakefield
Page 16 National Trust Photographic Library/ Paul Wakefield
Page 17 (both) National Trust Photographic Library/ Ian West
Page 18 National Trust Photographic Library/ Neil Campbell-Sharp
Page 19 National Trust Photographic Library/ David Levenson
Page 20 Imagen
Page 21 National Trust Photographic Library/ Ian Shaw
Page 22 National Trust Photographic Library/ Neil Campbell-Sharp
Page 23 National Trust Photographic Library/ John Hammond
Page 24 National Trust Photographic Library/ Ian West
Page 27 National Trust Photographic Library/ Neil Campbell-Sharp
Page 28 Imagen
Page 30 National Trust Photographic Library/ Colin Clarke
Page 33 National Trust Photographic Library/ Ian Shaw

DEVON
Pages 34-35 National Trust Photographic Library/ David Noton
Page 36 National Trust Photographic Library/ Derek Croucher
Page 37 (top) National Trust Photographic Library/ Lee Frost (bottom) National Trust Photographic Library/ David Noton
Page 38 National Trust Photographic Library/ Stephen Robson
Page 39 National Trust Photographic Library/ Andrew Butler
Page 40 National Trust Photographic Library/ Joe Cornish
Page 41 National Trust Photographic Library/ Joe Cornish
Page 42 Imagen
Page 43 National Trust Photographic Library/ Andreas von Einsiedel
Page 44 National Trust Photographic Library/ Paul Wakefield
Page 45 National Trust Photographic Library/ Ray Hallett
Page 47 Imagen

Page 48 Nature Photographers
Page 49 National Trust Photographic Library/ George Wright
Page 50 National Trust Photographic Library/ Joe Cornish
Page 51 National Trust Photographic Library/ Stephen Robson
Page 52 National Trust Photographic Library/ Joe Cornish
Page 53 National Trust Photographic Library/ Stephen Robson

THE MARCHES
Page 54-55 National Trust Photographic Library/ David Noton
Page 57 (top) National Trust Photographic Library/Andy Williams (bottom) National Trust Photographic Library/Rob Talbot
Page 58 National Trust Photographic Library/ Simon King/NaturePL
Page 59 Imagen
Page 60 National Trust Photographic Library/ Nick Meers
Page 61 NaturePL
Page 62 National Trust Photographic Library/ Ray Hallett
Page 63 National Trust Photographic Library/ Joe Cornish
Page 64 Nature Photographers
Page 65 Imagen
Page 66 National Trust Photographic Library/ Ray Hallett
Page 67 National Trust Photographic Library/ Roger Hickman
Page 68 National Trust Photographic Library/ Mike Williams
Page 69 Imagen

GARDEN OF ENGLAND
Pages 70-71 National Trust Photographic Library/ David Noton
Page 72 National Trust Photographic Library/ Andrew Butler
Page 73 (top) National Trust Photographic Library/ Derry Robinson (bottom) National Trust Photographic Library/Charlie Waite
Page 74 National Trust Photographic Library/ John Cancalosi/NaturePL
Page 75 National Trust Photographic Library/ Andrew Butler
Page 76 National Trust Photographic Library/ Ian Shaw
Page 78 National Trust Photographic Library/ D. Kjaer
Page 79 Imagen
Page 80 (both) National Trust Photographic Library/David Dixon
Page 81 Nature Photographers
Page 82 National Trust Photographic Library
Page 83 National Trust Photographic Library/ Ian Shaw
Page 84 National Trust Photographic Library/ Andreas von Einsiedel
Page 85 National Trust Photographic Library/ Ian Shaw
Page 86 National Trust Photographic Library/ Neil Campbell-Sharp
Page 87 National Trust Photographic Library/ Andreas von Einsiedel
Page 88 Nature Photographers
Page 89 Imagen

WESSEX

Pages 90-91 National Trust Photographic Library/ David Noton

Page 92 National Trust Photographic Library/ Nick Meers

Page 93 National Trust Photographic Library/ Joe Cornish

Page 95 (top) National Trust Photographic Library/Eric Crichton (bottom) National Trust Photographic Library/David Hall

Page 96 National Trust Photographic Library/ Joe Cornish

Page 97 National Trust Photographic Library/ Joe Cornish

Page 99 National Trust Photographic Library/ Joe Cornish

Page 100 Imagen

Page 101 National Trust Photographic Library/ Ian Shaw

Page 102 National Trust Photographic Library/ Stephen Robson

Page 103 National Trust Photographic Library/ John Hammond

Page 106 National Trust Photographic Library/ Stephen Robson

Page 107 National Trust Photographic Library/ Joe Cornish

Page 108 National Trust Photographic Library/ David Noton

Page 109 Frank Lane Picture Agency

FENS AND EAST ANGLIA

Pages 110-111 National Trust Photographic Library/ Ray Hallett

Page 113 (top) National Trust Photographic Library/John Miller (bottom) National Trust Photographic Library/Lee Frost

Page 114 Imagen

Page 117 National Trust Photographic Library/ Andreas von Einsiedel

Page 118 National Trust Photographic Library/ Niall Benvie/NaturePL

Page 120 National Trust Photographic Library/ Roy Fox

Page 122 National Trust Photographic Library/ Paul Wakefield

Page 123 National Trust Photographic Library/ John Miller

Page 124 Imagen

Page 126 Nature Photographers

Page 127 National Trust Photographic Library/ Joe Cornish

PEAK DISTRICT

Pages 128-129 National Trust Photographic Library/Joe Cornish

Page 131 (top) National Trust Photographic Library/Joe Cornish (bottom) National Trust Photographic Library/Will Curwen

Page 132 James Lynch/Foundation for Art, National Trust Photographic Library

Page 133 National Trust Photographic Library/ Stephen Robson

Page 135 Imagen

Page 136 National Trust Photographic Library/ Joe Cornish

Page 137 National Trust Photographic Library/ Joe Cornish

Page 139 National Trust Photographic Library/ Ray Hallett

Page 140 Frank Lane Picture Agency

Page 141 National Trust Photographic Library/ Joe Cornish

YORKSHIRE

Pages 142-143 National Trust Photographic Library/Joe Cornish

Page 145 (top) National Trust Photographic Library/Joe Cornish (bottom) National Trust Photographic Library/John Darley

Page 146 National Trust Photographic Library/ Mike Caldwell

Page 147 National Trust Photographic Library/ Joe Cornish

Page 149 Imagen

Page 150 National Trust Photographic Library/ David Noton

Page 152 National Trust Photographic Library/ Andrew Butler

Page 153 National Trust Photographic Library/ Andreas von Einsiedel

Page 154 National Trust Photographic Library/ Joe Cornish

Page 156 National Trust Photographic Library/ Neil Campbell-Sharp

Page 157 Imagen

Page 158 NaturePL

Page 159 Frank Lane Picture Agency

Page 160 Frank Lane Picture Agency

Page 161 National Trust Photographic Library/ Joe Cornish

Page 162 National Trust Photographic Library/ Joe Cornish

BORDERS

Pages 164-165 National Trust Photographic Library/Charlie Waite

Page 167 (top) National Trust Photographic Library/Andy Williams (bottom) Beamish Museum

Page 168 National Trust Photographic Library/ Stephen McCoy

Page 169 Duncan Davis

Page 170 National Trust Photographic Library

Page 171 National Trust Photographic Library/ Joe Cornish

Page 172 National Trust Photographic Library/ Mike Williams

Page 173 National Trust Photographic Library/ Dennis Gilbert

Page 175 Imagen

LAKE DISTRICT

Pages 176-177 National Trust Photographic Library/Derek Croucher

Page 179 (top) National Trust Photographic Library/David Noton (bottom) National Trust Photographic Library/Nick Meers

Page 180 National Trust Photographic Library/ Joe Cornish

Page 181 National Trust Photographic Library

Page 182 National Trust Photographic Library/ Andreas von Einsiedel

Page 183 National Trust Photographic Library/ David Levenson

Page 184 National Trust Photographic Library/ Joe Cornish

Page 186 National Trust Photographic Library

Page 187 Imagen

Page 189 National Trust Photographic Library

Page 190 National Trust Photographic Library/ Derek Croucher

Page 191 National Trust Photographic Library/ Lee Frost

Page 193 National Trust Photographic Library/ Joe Cornish

WALES

Pages 194-195 National Trust Photographic Library/Joe Cornish

Page 196 National Trust Photographic Library/ Andrew Butler

Page 197 (top) National Trust Photographic Library/Geoff Morgan (bottom) National Trust Photographic Library/Nick Carter

Page 198 National Trust Photographic Library/ David Noton

Page 199 Photolibrary Wales

Page 200 National Trust Photographic Library

Page 201 National Trust Photographic Library/ Andrea Jones

Page 202 Imagen

Page 203 National Trust Photographic Library/ Joe Cornish

Page 204 National Trust Photographic Library/ David Noton

Page 205 Imagen

Page 207 National Trust Photographic Library/ Charlie Waite

Page 208 National Trust Photographic Library/ Joe Cornish

Page 209 Nature Photographers

Page 210 National Trust Photographic Library/ Joe Cornish

Page 213 National Trust Photographic Library/ David Noton

NORTHERN IRELAND

Pages 214-215 National Trust Photographic Library/ Joe Cornish

Page 216 National Trust Photographic Library/ Paul Wakefield

Page 217 (top) National Trust Photographic Library/Mike Williams (bottom) Heritage Image Partnership

Page 219 Imagen

Page 220 Heritage Image Partnership

Page 221 National Trust Photographic Library/ Joe Cornish

Page 222 National Trust Photographic Library/ Joe Cornish

Page 223 National Trust Photographic Library/ Joe Cornish

Page 224 National Trust Photographic Library/ Jerry Harpur

Page 225 Nature Photographers

FARMING AND FOOD IN THE TWENTY-FIRST CENTURY

Page 226 National Trust Photographic Library/ Ian Shaw

Page 228 (top) National Trust Photographic Library/Ian Shaw (bottom) National Trust Photographic Library/David Levenson

Page 230 National Trust Photographic Library/ Ian Shaw

Page 232 (top) National Trust Photographic Library/Joe Cornish (bottom) National Trust Photographic Library/David Levenson

PICTURE CREDITS

Whip for Trifles.

Not quite 1/2 pint of Cream
1/2 pint Milk, and not
quite 1/2 pint Wine,
And the juice of 1 lemon
Sweeten to taste & the white
of 1 egg. Beat up to a good
froth, put it into a large
pan & with a whisk,
whisk it, and as the
froth rises take it off
with a Spoon & lay it on
a sieve to drain.

Soda Cake

1 lb Flour, 1/2 lb Currants,
6 oz Sugar, 1/2 pint Ale,
1 Tea Spoonful Soda
2 Eggs, & a little Spice
